The Grand National
Anybody's Race

The Grand National

Anybody's Race

Peter King

Quartet Books
London Melbourne New York

First published by Quartet Books Limited 1983
A member of the Namara Group
27/29 Goodge Street, London W1P 1FD

British Library Cataloguing in Publication Data

King, Peter
    The Grand National.
    1. Grand National—History
    798.4'5'0941   SF359.3.67

    ISBN 0-7043-2385-0

Typeset by MC Typeset, Chatham, Kent

Printed and bound in Great Britain at
The Camelot Press Ltd, Southampton

Contents

Illustrations

Acknowledgements

I am indebted to the many authors who have written about the Grand National, from early writers like Finch Mason to the *Grand National Commentary* by Pye which is still in the book-shops. It would be invidious to select from the various books on racing generally which have been helpful and from which I have quoted in my book. Heinemann kindly allowed me to quote extensively from *National Velvet* and I have also quoted from Dick Francis's autobiography, *The Barry Brogan Story* and from the reminiscences of other famous jockeys and trainers. The views of Lord Wigg and Mr Phil Bull have also been quoted at length. As regards the Jockey Club, the basic book is Robert Black's *The Jockey Club and its Founders,* and I have also quoted from Roger Mortimer's book – now out of print, alas.

The many friends to whom I am indebted include Philip, who was the first man I knew ever to set 'foot' on a horse; Graham for his encouragement, and Cherry for her thoughtful comments and for supplying the title.

Those who kindly helped with illustrations and photographs are listed on p. vi.

I have not written a preface, but I would briefly like to say with humility that those who can, do, and those who cannot, write about it. So I would have much preferred to have ridden in the National than to have been an author.

There are many famous courses
In the width of English ground
Where the steeplechasing horses
And the racing silks go round.
But it's Aintree, Aintree, Aintree,
Where the champion chasers run
Where there's courage to be tested
And there's glory to be won.

WILL OGILVIE

PART ONE

The History

1: Curtain Raiser

This is the story of how a club of one hundred members set about acquiring one of the world's greatest horseraces for only some half a million pounds of their own money, and how for this sum they also aimed to gain control of the racecourse on which it was run. (To be more precise, it is the story of how some fifty members of the club engaged in the enterprise because their fifty colleagues were either not interested in the project or were actively opposed to it.)

What they wished to acquire – the Grand National – is big business in the sense that the punters risk £30m on the race every year, thus out-betting every other British race, including the Derby, and producing a considerable profit for the bookmakers. In addition, the government takes £2¼m as tax from the betting, and this is ploughed back into racing, a factor of considerable interest to the one hundred members of the club which happens to control the racing industry in Britain. Another source of income arises from the vast television audience which the race attracts, making it of no little interest to sponsors, and ensuring that year after year it is likely to produce a profit of about a quarter of a million pounds.

The club is, of course, the Jockey Club – that strange British institution which is in charge of horseracing. For a club to manage racing is not unique, nor is it unique for a private group to own a racecourse. What makes the story unusual is that the

Jockey Club was attempting to gain control of a race which had always been in private hands without dipping into their own pockets very deeply, or making any inroads into the Club's funds. The plan was for the race to pass to them from a plasterer-turned-property-developer, who in turn had acquired it from an ex-chorus girl, who bought it from a peer of the realm who had been a Senior Steward of the Jockey Club. There might be some poetic justice in the Club getting the race therefore. A private club which publishes no accounts, and is one of the archetypal British institutions would seem the right and proper guardian of a race which is regarded by many as part of Britain's heritage.

Mirabel Topham was the ex-chorus girl who owned the racecourse and who, by forming a separate private company, had secured the rights to the race itself so that whoever owned the 260 acres of Aintree would not automatically be entitled to run the race there. And since everyone agreed that there was nowhere but Aintree where the race could rightly be staged, both racecourse and race had to be bought. For the Jockey Club to control the race (which in a sense they could be said to control anyway as they control all racing in Britain) seemed, if not inevitable, the best possible way of guaranteeing the Grand National's future.

There were, of course, other contenders for the prize. Ladbrokes the bookmakers, who had managed the race several years running, were said to be interested but could not agree a price with the vendor. Another interested party was the Levy Board, through whose hands passes most of the money which keeps British racing going. And a number of private individuals and public companies also made bids to purchase such a world-renowned name, rather like bidding for Rolls-Royce or the Royal Albert Hall, although their attempts came to nothing.

In the end the Jockey Club entered the field and, in 1983, for the first time organized the race which their one-time Senior Steward Lord Sefton had sold nearly forty years earlier to Mirabel Topham on the advice of his accountant, who gave it as his opinion that he would acquire more cash that way than by continuing to take rent, as his forebears had done for more than a hundred years. The question was, would the Jockey Club acquire the race in perpetuity? The word acquire is chosen carefully. The trust document for the purchase of Aintree and the race provides that the cash from the Grand National Appeal is to be transferred to a company wholly owned by the Injured Jockeys' Fund (or another racing charity) on condition that the company enters into a management agreement with Aintree Racecourse Ltd (a subsidiary of Racecourse Holdings Trust, itself a subsidiary of the Jockey Club) or another nominated company, to run the 1984 race and all subsequent races. This arm's-length arrangement would leave the Jockey Club with effective control.

2: Origins of the Jockey Club

The name of the Jockey Club is curious since it is not a club in the ordinary sense, nor are any jockeys members of it. The explanation is that in the eighteenth century it was common for owners to ride their own horses in matches, and the word 'jockey' was used for them as for other riders. When a group of such owners got together to form the Club it was natural that it should be given the name it still bears. The word 'club' also had a much wider meaning than it has today. No one knows precisely when the Club was formed but 1750 seems a reasonable guess, though it is not until 1752 that it is first mentioned in the *Sporting Calendar*.

Roger Mortimer in his book on the Jockey Club says 'there is not a shred of evidence to suggest that the Club was founded with any high-minded notion of governing or reforming the Turf. The character and habits of many of the Club's early members make such a suggestion ridiculous.'

The Star and Garter in Pall Mall where the Club first met was the scene of notable events, such as Lord Barrymore's offer to devour a live cat for a bet. It also met at the Corner, Hyde Park, where Mr Tattersall had his horse-mart, and eventually it was established in the premises of its agents, Messrs Weatherby, in Old Bond Street. The members in those days wore special dress that included boots and spurs, and a hundred years later the Stewards still wore a distinctive style of coat.

Newmarket was a great centre of racing and in order to acquire a meeting-place there, the Club obtained, in 1752, a plot of land on which it had constructed a building, known as the Coffee House, now the site of much more grandiose premises.

Rules governing the date of the Club's annual meeting and the appointment and tenure of Stewards were published in 1770: 'It was resolved that the Members should meet annually at dinner on the day preceding the King's birthday, that three members should be appointed Stewards [now it is eight] to commence their office on 4th June annually; one new Steward to be appointed every year on the 3rd of June, by the Steward who quits on that day, subject to the approbation of the Members of the Jockey Club then present.' The Stewards were given full powers to conduct racing affairs at Newmarket, and also all matters connected with the payments of stakes and forfeits. However, there was not much formality in these early days and it was not until sixty years later that a list of members was published.

The first well-known Steward of the Jockey Club was Sir Charles Bunbury, appointed when he was twenty-eight years old. Son of a Rector, MP for Suffolk, and then Chief Secretary for Ireland, he married a woman reputed to be the most beautiful in England – who ran away from him five years later. Despite Sir Charles's reputation during his lifetime as the driving-force and perpetual president of the Jockey Club and subsequently as the first dictator of the English Turf, no very clear picture of him as a man emerged. Under Bunbury's rule, the membership remained superior, if curiously behaved.

The Jockey Club has always had one of the Royal Family in membership, as it does today. The first was the unpopular William, Duke of Cumberland, second son of George II. He died in 1764 at the age of forty-four of 'sheer corpulence', but he had had a fundamental influence on the history of racing as he bred Eclipse, the greatest racehorse of all time, and Herod, and from these two horses and Matcham (who died aged thirty-three) the descent of every thoroughbred can be traced. Later, William IV became a member and remained one until he lost interest in racing after being struck in the eye by a ginger-nut thrown by one of the crowd at Ascot. While a member he presented the Jockey Club rooms at Newmarket with a silver salver on which was mounted one of the hooves of the Royal horse Eclipse, who was never beaten and was highly successful at stud, finally expiring at the age of twenty-six. Another of his hooves is at Windsor Castle. The Jockey Club also owns 'the Whip', thought to have been presented by Charles II; the present Whip has a wristband woven with hairs from Eclipse's tail.

Among the notable members of the early years of the Club was the Duke of Queensbury, known as 'Old Q' or the 'Star of Piccadilly'. He sat on his balcony in Piccadilly leering at the women passing below. Fearful stories were told of the unspeakable orgies in which the old roué took a prominent part, and also of the extraordinary means that he employed to stimulate his flagging sexual powers. Racing came second to sex as his abiding interest, and he became one of the best riders in the country, although his interest declined as he neared the age of ninety. Charles James Fox, another high-liver, was also a member at this time, and owned up to thirty racing horses.

An important battle in which the Club was involved in its early days was the publication of the *Racing Calendar*. In the 1770s Mr James Weatherby conspired with one of the partners publishing the *Sporting Calendar* to expropriate and conceal the copies of the book just before publication, so that subscribers could not obtain their volumes, and when his partner suddenly died, Weatherby boldly issued his first volume of the *Racing Calendar*, a shameless crib of the *Sporting Calendar*, which in due course became the official organ of the Jockey Club. Weatherby's position as Keeper of the Match Book, a post which became hereditary in the Weatherby family, gave him an advantage over any rival, and gradually the *Racing Calendar* became the voice of the Club, which purchased it in the 1980s, although Weatherby's continue to issue it on its behalf.

The membership continued to include colourful characters. For example, there was the twelfth Earl of Derby who gave his name to the race (as well as to the Oaks, named after his house). Lord Derby married an actress, Nellie Farren, after a ten-year courtship which Boswell described as an attachment 'as fine as anything I have ever seen'. His cook complained that the late suppers her company occasioned were 'killing him'. The Earl nonchalantly requested that he include a fixed sum on the bill for 'wear and tear of life'. Another member who made a strange marriage was Sir John Lade, who wed Letty Smith, former mistress of Sixteen Strong Jack, a highwayman hanged at Tyburn.

A noted event in Jockey Club lore occurred in 1790, when Sam Chifney, riding the Prince of Wales's Escape, was accused of cheating by the Newmarket Steward, Sir Charles Bunbury, who effectively blacked him from riding the Prince's horses. The Prince gave Chifney 200 guineas a year for life, but HRH never patronized Newmarket again. He told Chifney's son that the Jockey Club has 'treated your father and me very badly; I won't run there'. Chifney died at the age of fifty-two, bankrupt and broken in health and spirit.

The Club's right to warn an individual off from Newmarket was established by law on a number of occasions during the early 1800s on the basis that it had been tenant of the grounds since the 1750s. By 1807 it was also publishing reports of 'cases' it had judged. In 1817 the Club imposed an order about stake money and two years later a tax on those using Newmarket Heath; virtually the whole of the Heath was now in their hands. In 1843, the decision was made to take no cognizance of matters concerning betting – as more and more of the Club's time had been taken up with wrangles. Betting disputes were now settled by Tattersall's Committee, chaired by a member of the Jockey Club. In 1870 there was a ruling that neither the programme nor the results of a race should be published unless it was advertised to be subject to the Rules of Racing. Any owner, jockey or official who took part in an unrecognized meeting would be disqualified. By these means and others, the Club gradually extended its power over racing and by the last quarter of the nineteenth century, not only were jockeys, trainers and officials licensed by the Club, but so were the racecourses. Fifty years earlier, the Club had been far less powerful, although they were already trying to extend their influence, as had been evident in the 1830s when a notice in the *Calendar* stated that the Jockey Club 'have no authority to extend their Rules and Orders to any other place; although they have, for the sake of uniformity and certainty, recommended the adoption of the same Rules to the Stewards of other races'. The object of this notice was clearly to bring all race meetings under a unified control and to place the remainder, which failed to comply, beyond the pale of recognized authority. The policy was of the greatest benefit to racing, and from this comparatively small beginning came eventually reciprocal agreements with the Turf authorities of almost every civilized country in the world.

The dominating Jockey Club figure on the English turf between 1836 and 1846 was Lord George Bentinck, a strong character who developed the method of starting races which has led to the modern 'gate'. He also devised the principle of differently priced enclosures, with amenities varying according to the price of entry. He invented the saddling enclosure, developed Goodwood and helped plan the new Derby course. He fought fraud – such as the running of substitute horses – fearlessly. Despite all this, he was a gambler on a very large scale and to ensure that he would win, adopted many 'strategems and manoeuvres'. Charles Greville wrote of him 'if everybody knew of all his tricks and artifices, what a rogue he would be thought . . . He has made for himself a peculiar code of morality and honour, and what he has done, he thinks he has a right to do, that the game at which he plays warrants deceit and falsehood . . . In short, while he is thundering away against poor low-lived rogues for the villainies they have committed, he had been doing the same things which high-minded men (like his father for instance) who do not split hairs and make nice distinctions on questions of honour, would think nearly if not quite as discreditable and reprehensible.' He gave up racing for politics and was very chagrined when Disraeli came into the House and told him that a horse he had once owned had just won the Derby. He summed up his own character when he said 'I don't pretend to know much, but I can judge men and horses.'

After Bentinck, the fame of the Jockey Club was in the hands of Admiral Henry John Rous, who ruled the Turf from 1846 to 1877. He was an impetuous man, who was addicted to writing letters to the newspaper before fully acquainting himself with the facts of the matter about which he was writing. He was an expert on the Rules of Racing and owned the famous Stubbs painting of Gimcrack which he bequeathed to the Club.

About ten years after Rous's election, the fourteenth Earl of Derby wrote to the Stewards of the Jockey Club as follows:

My Lords,
It has become a subject of general observations and regret,

that the number of men of station and fortune who support the Turf is gradually diminishing, and that an increasing proportion of horses in training is in the hands of persons in an inferior position, who keep them not for the purposes of sport but for the purposes of gambling . . . I venture to think that it is your duty, as Stewards of the Jockey Club, to exercise a wholesome influence upon the character and respectability of the Turf.

Rous set about the task of 'exercising a wholesome influence' and within two or three years the Club was so firmly established that a bill introduced into Parliament to control racing was by common consent withdrawn at the Club's instigation. He did much to establish law and order on the racecourses. 'Those who take for granted the well-ordered racecourses of today have little notion of the roughness, violence and downright villainy that were a commonplace at any race meetings in the mid-Victorian era . . . *The Times* was not far off the mark when it said that a large portion of the sporting world was identical with the vilest section of the community.' Although the Jockey Club was slow to warn off some of the vilest, 'on the whole it [the Club] has served the Turf remarkably well', wrote Roger Mortimer in his book.

Rous had a highly developed sense of business and succeeded in raising the income from Newmarket, which was £3,000 a year when he became Steward in 1838, to £18,000 by the time of his death. He also became the public handicapper and carried out his duties with great *élan*, feeling very strongly that jockeys should be kept in their place – that place being a comparatively humble one. For twenty-five years his word in legitimate racing was law, although unfortunately neither Rous nor the Club did anything to stem the abuses of steeplechasing at this time. Steeplechasing was not considered 'legitimate'. Those who were warned off Newmarket and flat racing could, and did, enter steeplechasing. People suspended at one steeplechase could appear at another. A standard book on the subject said 'As the sport grew popular, it grew infamous; it was indeed the refuge of all outcasts, human and equine, from the legitimate turf.' Finally, in 1863 Weatherby's *Calendar* published the 'Grand National Steeplechase Rules', but Rous was not satisfied and wrote off to *The Times*, referring to steeplechasing as an extraneous branch of horseracing. The same year a National Hunt Committee was set up, membership being from the Jockey Club. It was self-elected and had no formal status. Within a year it was asked to adjudicate in a dispute. By the end of 1865, the Club decided that there should be a formal and separate governing body for steeplechasing and the Grand National Hunt Steeplechase Committee of sixteen members was established. This was seen by some as moving steeplechasing away from the hunting fraternity and more and more into the hands of racing – that is, flat racing. It was to be nearly one hundred years before the Jockey Club and National Hunt were to come together.

After Rous's death, there were, happily, other men of character to provide leadership of the Club over prolonged periods. From 1882 to 1928 the dominant role was played by the Earl of Durham, although it was said that in his time it needed no particular brilliance to shine in the Jockey Club – like a diamond necklace in a heap of coke. In 1887 there was a famous libel suit about a race between Durham and Sir George Chetwynd. Sir George was awarded a farthing damages so resigned from the Club and retired from racing. Among Durham's achievements was the introduction of the starting-gate, a campaign for racing to continue during the 1914–18 war, and the introduction of further security arrangements to protect the public on racecourses.

The Jockey Club was reluctant to introduce certain innovations and it sometimes needed a kick to move it into the present era. Doping was a case in point. As early as 1812, a tout had been publicly hanged for administering arsenic to racehorses and by the turn of the century doping had become such a scandal that the Jockey Club was asked to intervene. It refused. The Hon. George Lambton, who trained for Lord Derby, told the Stewards that he would dope five unreliable horses to show what they would do in a race. Four of the five horses won their races, and the fifth came second. Previously not one had shown any form. The Club then woke up to the dangers and decided that those who administered or caused drugs to be administered would be warned off.

Despite its shortcomings, 'Criticism of the Jockey Club as an institution is not however of sufficient proportion or influence to place the authority and status of the Club in jeopardy,' says Roger Mortimer, and this was to some extent because few changes were made in the type of member now elected to the Club. For example, Lord Rank, the miller and cinema magnate who was elected when he was seventy years old, was described as 'a member of the commercial middle class', and membership remained predominantly Establishment, with an occasional incursion into the famous, such as Sir Winston Churchill who became a member, as his father, Randolph Churchill, had been before him, although he was not passionate about racing.

The major change in membership occurred at the beginning of 1969 when the Jockey Club and the National Hunt Committee finally amalgamated, and flat racing and steeplechasing combined their interests. This doubled the membership from fifty to one hundred, but the change of membership was an increase in size and not in character. A conservative wrote 'the day is surely near when a sport like racing in which so much money is involved, can be controlled no longer by what is basically a social club drawn from a very small circle'. Weatherby's still provided a large part of the secretariat for this 'social club'. The family connection had begun in rather a questionable way, as we have seen, but by this century all this was behind them and they claimed to be, and were, part of the Establishment. The Rothschild Commission on Gambling comments: 'It is a curious but perhaps appropriate feature of the Jockey Club that its secretariat should be bred rather than recruited in the usual manner.'

Stewards of the Jockey Club only hold office for three years; the continuity of government is supplied by the members of the Weatherby family whose role in racing had been compared to that of 'those invaluable civil servants who serve and advise members of the Cabinet. As a family, the Weatherbys possess the admirable qualities of the best type of civil servant, to wit: experience, discretion, loyalty, a dislike of publicity, and, in most cases, a Winchester education. Like most civil servants, they are not infrequently criticised . . . over the somewhat rigid and old-fashioned manner in which their business is said to be conducted, and in an alleged tendency to say no.'

We shall see that the last of the Weatherbys to be the Club's Secretary, Simon, claimed that he had tried to drag the Club into the nineteenth century, if not into the twentieth. He did not succeed in uniting the two wings of the Jockey Club, the Flat and the National Hunt, and despite the merger, each continued to espouse its own class of racing, little or no enthusiasm being shown by the Flat people for the Grand National Appeal.

The schism went back a long way; listen to Mr Sponge commenting on the subject in 1800:

'Steeplechases are generally crude, ill-arranged things. Few sportsmen will act as stewards a second time; while the victim to the popular delusion of patronising our national sports considers – like gentlemen who have served the office of sheriff or churchwarden – that once in a lifetime is enough, hence, there is always the air of amateur actorship about them. There is always something wanting or forgotten. Either they forget the ropes, or they forget the scales, or they forget the weights, or they forget the bell or – more commonly still – some of the parties forget themselves. Farmers, too, are easily satisfied with the benefits of an irresponsible mob careering over their farms, even though some of them are attired in the miscellaneous garb of hunting and racing costume. Indeed, it is just this mixture of two sports that spoils both; steeplechasing being neither hunting nor racing. It has not the wild excitement of the one, nor the accurate calculating qualities of the other. The very horses have a peculiar air about them – neither hunters or hacks, nor yet exactly racehorses. Some of them, doubtless are fine, good-looking, well-conditioned animals, but the majority are lean, lanky, abused, sunken-eyed, woe-begone, iron-marked, desperately-abused brutes, lacking all the lively energy that characterises the movements of the up-to-the mark hunter. In the early days of steeplechasing a popular fiction existed that the horses were hunters, and grooms and fellows used to come nicking and grinning up to masters of hounds at checks and critical times, requesting them to note that they were out, in order to ask for certificates of the horses having been "regularly hunted", a species of regularity than which nothing could be more irregular. That nuisance, thank goodness, is abated. A steeplechaser now generally stands on his own merits; a change for which sportsmen may be thankful.'

3: The Jockey Club Today

As late as 1969 *The Times* recorded that the current Senior Steward, Sir Randle Fielden, was looking to the City for members nowadays, and the election of Sir Harry Benson, it said, a senior partner in a firm of accountants, was 'an indication of the way things were going'. They did not go that way for long and today there are precious few 'City' men as members who would not have been able to enjoy membership under earlier criteria. These criteria are, of course, unspoken, if not unspeakable. To be one of the hundred-odd members (double the membership of earlier times due to the introduction of the National Hunt or steeplechasing fraternity) it is necessary to be invited to join and to be able to pay the £100 subscription (double the figure ten years ago). The critics may nevertheless be exaggerating the difficulties, particularly one who asserted 'You have to be a relative of God, and a close one at that.' So did the bookmaker reported to have said that the members were the sort of people 'likely to shoot you before breakfast'. 'Yet these days,' wrote *The Times*, 'the question most likely to be asked is not "Who was your father?" but "What can you do for racing?" '

It was Simon Weatherby, Secretary until January 1983, who said of the membership: 'Up to the war, it was highly aristocratic, lived behind closed doors. Did what it pleased. But now we have an era of consultation. Everyone is consulted exhaustively about everything, and the Jockey Club, rather like the Vatican, is the last port of call.' The membership, too, is traditional no longer. 'People are not still chosen because they are socially OK but because they are of cast-iron integrity and prepared to provide both expertise and time.'

He was making the point that the critics are wrong to say that all the members of the Club were educated at Eton and Christ Church, followed by a spell in the Guards. Any analysis of the membership shows this is false, although Eton is the predominant educational establishment. The Army, too, is the major post-scholastic activity, with 2 captains, 6 majors, 2 lt.-colonels, 4 brigadiers and 4 assorted generals still using their titles, and almost all the others, from the Senior Steward downwards, having had a spell in the military. Of the membership of 108, seventy-six either have titles, or military nomenclature, or were at Eton or Harrow.

This military character continues into the permanent staff of the Club, many of whom are recruited from unemployed ex-Army officers. For example there are about a hundred 'Officials under the Rules of Racing' who look after discipline on the racecourses of whom forty use military titles and many of the others no doubt could but don't. Of the 250 or so Stewards under Jockey Club Rules over half are titled or have military embellishments to their names.

Of the members who do not fit the pattern which the critics so enjoy describing, there are the Patrons, the Queen and the Queen Mother; the honorary members HRH Prince Philip (not much interested in racing); HRH the Prince of Wales; Brigadier H.J.L. Green CBE (the Director of Security); Mr Raymond Guest and Mr Paul Mellon, the two rich Americans; Sir Gordon Richards, the famous jockey; and Mr P.M. Weatherby, one of the older Weatherbys. Among the ordinary members, the most senior is the Deputy Senior Steward, Mr Louis Freedman, who bought the Beech House Stud from Lady Sassoon and the Cliveden Stud on the death of Lord Astor following a highly successful career on the board of Land Securities, the property developers. On retirement, he put his business acumen at the disposal of the Jockey Club.

Robert Sangster, founder and chairman of Vernons Pools, was elected in 1972, Sir Freddie Laker was elected in 1979 at the height of his fame, and in 1982 at the nadir of his misfortunes he was serving on the Administration and Finance Committee of the Club. Lord Weinstock was elected in 1978, his father-in-law, Sir Michael Sobell in 1971, and the Hon. David Sieff, of Marks and Spencer, in 1977. Of the five lady members, one, a Dame, says she is not an unlikely member because 'after all, I have been in racing politics some time and have always owned some modest horses'.

As we have seen, there was a time when the members of the Jockey Club wore a kind of uniform. Today they do not do so, but they have a distinctive air, none the less. Striped suits, a gold chain from the buttonhole to the top pocket, and a striped shirt. The tie will be held to the shirt at belly-button level by a gold stock-pin. The tie will not be a Club tie ('No one wears a Club tie nowadays,' said a member) and it is preferable to wear Gucci shoes rather than the brogue variety.

The Club is not a club in the normal sense, like White's. The Turf Club fulfils this role for the racing world. It has, however, club facilities of a sort at Newmarket which will be described later. Its main activities are nothing less than the control of British racing from its offices at Portman Square, two floors rented from the Brewers' Society, with a small staff which not only administers racing, but also houses the following:

The Racecourse Owners' Association
The Racecourse Association Ltd
Permit Trainers' Association
National Trainers' Federation
Racecourse Security Services Ltd
The Thoroughbred Breeders' Association

Also at No. 42 Portman Square is the home of Racecourse Holdings Trust Ltd, the company running the racecourses owned by the Jockey Club, and of other bodies which feature in the story.

The members do not do much to dilute the image of naked power backed by wealth. Lord Leverhulme, a one-time Senior Steward, when asked if financial constraints would not drive trainers out of racing, replied 'Oh, they can always own greyhounds.' And Lord Howard de Walden admitted that he didn't need £2m that badly when he turned down that figure offered for his two-year-old colt.

Critics of the Jockey Club often complain that as a private club, it does not publish its accounts, and this is unsatisfactory for a body which controls racing and so many of the leading racecourses. Such complaints are somewhat misleading, as are the guesses made at the Club's income. In 1969 *The Times* claimed that it totalled probably about £45,000, but this must have been a long way off the mark if the Club's principal subsidiaries are taken into account.

The point is that the subsidiaries do publish accounts, but no one has analysed them. Had they done so, the critics would have found details of the Club's properties at Newmarket, on the one hand, and very detailed figures for the individual racecourses, on the other, showing exactly how much it costs annually to operate the courses, and how much is received by way of income. Not all companies are so open with their figures.

The Jockey Club has two substantial subsidiaries, one Newmarket Estates and Property Company Ltd, which in the 1960s had taken over the properties at Newmarket, and the other, Racecourse Holdings Trust Ltd, which operated all the racecourses owned or run by the Jockey Club (including Newmarket).

The directors of Newmarket Estates were, as one might expect, all members of the Jockey Club and the shareholders likewise (although others were permitted). Provision was made in the Articles of Association that if a special resolution were passed to the effect that a shareholder was not a person having at heart the best interests of the sport and industry of horseracing, then he shall cease to be a member. Shares are not transferable and cease upon death.

In the accounts for 31 December 1981 (the last available) the Chairman, Sir Philip Oppenheimer of de Beers, said that the profits for the year were £288,330 before tax, compared with £227,263 in 1980. In both years this included substantial profit from the sale of fixed assets; in 1981 £241,032 was raised mainly from the sale of fourteen acres at Newmarket to Middle Eastern consortiums for the erection of new training stables. Incidentally such a sale must have been a shock to the early critics who described Newmarket as 'miles and miles of buggerall'. This sale improved the liquid assets position of Newmarket Estates to the extent that the Chairman was able to report that these totalled just over £1m. There were, he said, a record number of 2,000 horses on the heath and 'a quiescent Trainers' Federation'.

The fixed assets totalled over £6½m, having been revalued upwards from about £2m in 1978. The large surplus on these revaluations was transferred to capital reserves, and the accounts state 'the directors have at the present time no intention of disposing of these assets'. This comment was made in 1978, but the sale of a few acres for £200,000 to the Arabs in 1981 and a similar sale in the previous year indicates that they were not adamant on this point.

Again, in late 1978 a local contractor converted the Newmarket Chambers into seven flats and nineteen bedrooms, and the former were sold off. The accounts also state that Newmarket Estates has valued at over £1m its paintings, prints and silver, which are not recorded in the accounts except at nil value 'as the directors have no intention of disposing of them' although in the previous year, proceeds from sales which included profits on the sale of a painting were recorded in the accounts.

So it seems as if there were substantial liquid sums available to the Jockey Club through its subsidiary Newmarket Estates should it wish to help buy the National. Of course, the viability of the valuations of the land at Newmarket may be questioned, and there might be considerable difficulty in disposing of land there, or at any rate of disposing of pieces of land at the kind of price paid by the Arab group.

And for all the fuss that was to be made when the Club was asked for a guarantee for the Appeal, the accounts also show that Newmarket Estates did guarantee the other Jockey Club subsidiary, RHT Ltd, to the tune of £100,000 and deposited the deeds to certain Newmarket properties in support of the guarantees – and had charges on RHT Ltd to offset them. There was also an unsecured loan to RHT Ltd of £250,000 at the same period.

All this indicates that while the Jockey Club may (or may not) have money of its own, its richest subsidiary, Newmarket Estates, could at a pinch have provided some money towards saving a national heritage like the Grand National had it so desired. But it did not so desire. Why not?

The other Jockey Club company, almost equally large on paper, Racecourse Holding Trust Ltd, was also controlled by the Jockey Club which held ninety per cent of the shares. Three directors out of eight were not members of the club. It operated its racecourses through subsidiary companies, all consolidated in the accounts, the most recent being Haydock Park, purchased at the bargain basement price of £427,055.

In the year ending 31 December 1981, RHT Ltd carried forward retained profits of £683,791, about £100,000 up on the previous year. An important factor regarding this subsidiary however is that the Horserace Betting Levy Board's grants (for racecourse improvements) were very substantial, about £2.7m in 1981 and a similar amount in 1980. Thus RHT Ltd has received considerable sums from the Levy Board which were repayable in the event of racing being discontinued at the course concerned. These were interest-free loans, although there were also grants. The question of selling off a racecourse and using the money for another purpose (e.g. buying Aintree) would not therefore arise. For this reason, therefore, the considerable assets of RHT Ltd are not available in the ordinary sense that they would be available to the directors of a business. And another question – are the assets valued at a realistic figure, bearing in mind that there must be a limited number of people who wish to buy a racecourse?

In short, RHT Ltd, despite its sizeable assets, did not have large sums of ready money with which to buy Aintree, unless, like Haydock, it had been on offer at a bargain price.

Now to return to the question why the Newmarket Company did not take steps to provide some financial contribution to the saving of Aintree. One possible answer is that a majority of the board of directors were flat-racing, not steeplechasing, supporters, and, far from wishing to spend money on Aintree, some of them may well have thought it would be better lost than saved. At the same time the board was in a sense only representative of the Jockey Club, so they would be expressing not only a personal view, if they were negative, but also one that represented a substantial body of Club opinion. They could hardly go against opinion in the Club.

Another possible reason might be that they felt it prudent to keep such assets to support the activities of RHT Ltd, since the latter operated with grants from the Horserace Levy Board. However, had this been the case, and they were worried on this score, then an approach could have been made to the Levy Board to see what its view would be to selling off some of Newmarket's liquid assets to help save Aintree. No such approach was made.

It is therefore difficult to escape the conclusion that the Club and its subsidiaries had no intention of using its own money to buy Aintree, or help to save Aintree, if a small number of members, and a large number of non-members, could be persuaded to give to the Appeal instead. Control of Aintree would then go to Racecourse Holdings Trust, the Jockey Club subsidiary, without a hand being placed in the Club pocket.

No analysis of a club would be complete without some description of how it feels to belong to it. There is a difficulty here, however, because the Jockey Club is not one of your London clubs in any sense. Indeed, the members, when describing themselves in *Who's Who* or similar self-advertising material, often use the indicator: Clubs – Jockey (Newmarket) and we shall see why it is Newmarket that is indicated.

The fact is that members are not particularly encouraged to visit Portman Square, which in any event, will lead to disappointment on first sight, and on second. The name Portman Square conjures up, does it not, a vision of leafy gardens surrounded by elegant Georgian façades, if not of hansom cabs? Not a bit of it. No. 42 is an architectural monstrosity, only slightly less disgraceful than the Portman Building Society next door, and the Churchill Hotel to the west. All were once graceful Georgian, indeed Adam, buildings, like the Courtauld Institute which survives to the north. But the present owners of No. 42 were pleased to be able to bash down an Adam's house in 1963 and commission architects James Ralph, to replace it. It belongs to the Brewers' Society, who are the Club's landlords. Internally it is divided into those glass-partitioned barracks typical of government buiidings from Moscow to Cardiff, with cream-painted walls and a pervading gloom which the sun seems never to penetrate. Automatic coffee-vending machines and pictures of the Queen Mother decorate the corridors. A member if he is lucky, having put his car in the basement garage, might penetrate to the third-floor offices of the Senior Steward, which are more elegant than those which house the permanent staff. The current incumbent, Lord Manton, had some of the Newmarket pictures brought to London where he claims to spend more time because 'We've got to get more involved in the corridors of power. Try to persuade the Government they are taking too much out of the sport.' But unless he has a job to do, or an inquiry to attend, the member will find nothing to detain him. There is nowhere to sit, and the luncheon room upstairs is reserved for the Senior Steward, the Weatherbys, one or two other officials and visiting Stewards.

Visiting the Club at Newmarket is a different thing altogether. The member entering the Rooms (as they are called) would have a genuine feeling of membership in a society of equals whose main purpose, said one of the first historians of the Club, 'so far as one can see, was to have a good time'. And the members keep themselves to themselves in the process – the discreet notice on the entrance says 'Jockey Club – PRIVATE'.

Two distinguished architects of the 1930s – not a distinguished period of our architectural heritage – tampered with the façade of the building to such an extent that there is little of the feeling of the 1770s left about it. Indeed a member might be excused, on first sight, for believing that he was entering a rather posh branch of Lloyds Bank. That is unfair – there is nearly half an acre of raked gravel to one side – and raked gravel is rarer than caviare nowadays – and to its left something about the lines of the building that clearly indicate the genius of Henry Holland, who also did Brooks's Club in St James's and the first Brighton Pavilion. The 1930s team roofed in behind the arcade forming a new internal room, which however still has windows from the coffee room looking into it. The Betting Court, in front of the façade, was originally paved with cobbles from Yarmouth beach, so the new architects followed the Regency marine theme by obtaining their supply of cobblestones from Brighton. They also added many amusing allusions to the purpose of the Rooms – a half moon crowning the lamp-standards is believed to be a reference to the famous horse Eclipse, whose gold-mounted hoof is within, and the handle of the main door is modelled as a horse's head. But where the new architects went badly astray was in topping the lot with an ornate clock tower, which has nothing to do with Holland's original design.

However, it will not do to dally any longer in the High Street, carping at the architectural infelicities of the 1930s, because once inside one will immediately have a feeling not only of 'Here is where it all began' but also of 'Here is what it is all about'.

Entering the pastel-coloured Rooms, the member's first stop will be to read Edward VII's carefully handwritten Christmas card to his horse Persimmon, which won the Derby. Looking about him, the impression would not be one of exceptional wealth and affluence – the Rooms have been described as 'very modest and unassuming'. They are, after all, on the site of a former Coffee House and bang next door to My Lord Rockingham's stables, and it was by acquiring a fifty-year lease on the Coffee House that the Club began its long occupancy. The Club was even thought modest by an eighteenth-century essayist. 'The Coffee Room so modestly turns its back upon the street, as if to shun the public view in silent retirement . . . large, plain and elegantly neat but not grand enough methinks for the noble company that frequent it. I think the place admirably suited to the intention of stillness, social amusement and wise discourse for which it was doubtless designed. Those boxes are, I daresay, purposely divided to avoid the confusion and hurry of a general mixture of company, and to receive a select party of half a dozen gentlemen who, leaving the bustle and hurry of the Turf, and the tide of anxious passions that attends it, meet here to unbend the mind with calm and amusing conversation.' Irony here?

In addition to members of the Jockey Club, the building houses members of the Jockey Club Rooms. These are limited to 300 in number, each elected by two other members, and one of these is a member of the Jockey Club proper. These members of the Rooms, as distinct from members of the Jockey Club, have the use of all the rooms in the building, with the exception of the Club's meeting-room, and the Club's dining-room. This latter room is reserved at breakfast times during race weeks for the Jockey Club, and all members eat there including the Royal family if they so wish. Members of the Rooms breakfast elsewhere. The Subscription Rooms Club, a separate group referred to as a 'Poor Man's Jockey Club', was not a successful venture and has now been given over to a National Horseracing Museum.

To return to our tour, on the mantelpiece of the Arcade room in a glass case is the celebrated Whip whose thong is composed of hair from the immortal Eclipse, and the plait which passes over the rider's wrist is made of hairs from the great horse's tail. Members can challenge to 'hold' it. From the Arcade room we pass to the new coffee room, and on to the card rooms and the dining-room which looks out on to the modern gardens through a large bay window. This has two fireplaces, over one of which is a splendid equestrian portrait of Isinglass by a Bavarian artist, and several of his other paintings of Derby winners cover the room. A feature which indicates the conviviality of the Club in Regency times is a mahogany wine cooler which holds up to ten magnums. But the crowning glory, centrepiece of the forty-two-foot long dining-table, is Eclipse's hoof, resting on an ornate gold salver.

The card rooms are somewhat plainer in appearance, more like the rooms of a Harley Street physician, although there is a grander chandelier than will be likely to be found in Harley Street. Here is to be seen another distinguished whip, which was carried by the famous Fred Archer, and the room holds memorabilia of the noted Admiral Rous, including the picture he gave the Club, estimated to be worth £1m today, painted by George Stubbs with help from Hogarth who, it is said, obliged with the figures. The horse is alleged to be Gimcrack, after whom the Gimcrack Club and Gimcrack Stakes were named.

In the other card room can be found the portrait of the other famous Jockey Club Steward, Lord George Bentinck, rather a stern figure, who gave up horses for politics, somewhat to his regret.

The committee room is also elegantly festooned with photographs and pictures of members, and is where the occasional formal meetings of the Club take place. Finally there are a number of individual rooms for officials of the club, notably Weatherby's rooms and the Stewards' rooms. The Stewards' room used to be the scene of disciplinary hearings or carpetings, but these 'private courts' now take place in London. Among the rich and rare pots and plate is the Goodwood Cup which journalist and novelist Edgar Wallace presented to the Jockey Club after successfully bidding for it at the sale of the Duke of Richmond plate.

Lying well back from these main rooms are the suites which

were erected in 1882 for the Prince of Wales, and used by him when King Edward, and by his son King George, and the other fifty-six bedrooms for the members' use. Simply but elegantly furnished, these rooms will provide a member with the ultimate feeling of belonging. Lying in his bed, he will be disposed to dwell on his own well-being and will have no sympathy for the fellow who described Newmarket 'as miles and miles of bugger-all'. On the following morning, after breakfast, the member heading for the Heath will finally be able to distinguish himself by affixing to his coat that discreet metal badge, engraved with his name, which admits him to any racecourse in the country.

All this is to be had for a hundred pounds sub. It is, of course, not a matter of mere money but of other qualities that ensure election to the Club, which finally requires the securing of at least nine nominations, and avoiding the two little black balls which are so fatal and probably so final.

4: A Tour of the Course

Strictly speaking, Aintree seems to be called Liverpool race-course, although the Jockey Club has registered a subsidiary called Aintree Racecourse Ltd to run the race there.

The National course is 4 miles 856 yards in length, bearing in mind that the riders go round twice. It is now all turf (except for the Melling Road) rather than a mixture of turf, plough, soil and turf, and even wheat, which was the terrain in the early days of the race. The fences are all artificial, and their unique, particular characteristic is that on most there is some inches difference in the level of the take-off and landing side, and this can be as much as 2½ feet. These are known as drop fences, and originated in the natural levels of the fields from which the course was made up. The distance over which the race is run has also varied, but has not been changed since 1890. In the early days, many spectators followed on horseback. For others, there was a beautiful layer-cake grandstand. As the race grew in prominence, the number of spectators grew accordingly and sometime in the late 1800s the old grandstand was replaced by the tiered and pillared structure, still there today, however tenuously.

In the early days there was no inside rail or running-rail, and the fences were uneven in height. The story goes that a rider walking the course before the race hit on the idea of putting a piece of paper to mark the easiest part of each fence, so that he would see, as he approached it, where to jump at its lowest. Alas, he was observed in his stratagem by a fellow competitor who moved the pieces of paper to the most difficult point of the fences.

In 1863/4 the fences were reduced in size. They then included hurdles for about a quarter of the total obstacles.

The next major alteration to the fences was in 1961, when they were sloped away on the take-off side so giving the horse an extra couple of feet to gain height to get over them.

The first time round the National is over sixteen fences, and the second time round over fourteen. The start is in front of the stands and immediately the course crosses the Melling Road, which on non-racing days is a public road. All fences must be a minimum of 4 ft 6 in. high except the Water Jump. They are a fearsome sight, being hand-built from hawthorn (very thick, spiky stumps) and dressed with spruce, fir or gorse. A horse hitting one of these fences does so at 25–30 mph.

Dick Francis describes Aintree as a 'flat and difficult' course and says the difficulty lies in the varying state of the going when it has been raining. The racecourse proper remains soft, while out in the country it drains quickly and dries quickly. By 'out in the country' Francis means where the National course leaves the Flat course. Francis says that in very dry weather, the rarely used turf out in the country remains springy, while the racecourse is inclined to be firm.

Francis describes how galloping towards Becher's the horses in front disappear as they jump the 'drop fence' and then just the caps of the jockeys bob into sight as they ride on.

'On no other course is this feature so constant and so marked, and it is the drops taken at racing pace, more than the actual size of the fences, which are the chief hazard at Aintree . . . A slight but not exaggerated drop is helpful to a horse, for it gives him extra time to stretch his feet and before he touches the ground.'

Becher's is the sixth fence down the long straight and Francis says it should be jumped at a fair speed. 'One's only hope at Becher's is to clear the brook completely.'

The seventh does not have a ramp-like approach to the fence, so the horse must stand back for it to jump, says Francis.

The next is the Canal Turn, a right-angled turn immediately after the fence. Many riders by jumping the fence at an angle have difficulties and come to grief here.

Valentine's is a brook – indeed the same brook as that which used to be at Becher's. It needs the same courage as Becher's.

Francis says the next three fences require 'no more than ordinary care' before arriving at the Melling Road.

He then describes the Chair, in front of the stands, as the most difficult of the whole course, because of its height and spread and its formidable appearance. 'Mercifully, after the extra effort required to jump it, there is hardly any drop to complicate the landing.' John Hislop agrees. 'The obstacle,' he says, 'that makes my heart beat fastest as one nears it is the Chair. It stands up against the skyline, grim, tall and formidable, the rail before it reminding one of the veritable moat that it guards, and the fence itself seeming as impenetrable as a prison wall.'

The Chair is so called because there was an official on a chair at the end of the fifteenth fence nearest to the run-in, whose job was to retire those horses which had not reached him by the time the winner passed the winning-post. They were described as 'distanced' and this was the origin of the expression 'to win by a distance'. The pedestal on which the chair stood is still there.

The end of the first circuit is the Water Jump, fence No. 16, which in 1852 was described as a 'very large but perfectly fair jump'. Francis calls it the easiest of them all. The race then swings off to the left past the winning-post, under the starting-gate and off to the seventeenth fence, so beginning the second circuit by jumping a second time over the original first fence.

The second circuit is the same as the first, but misses out the Chair and the Water Jump. It has been said that if a horse is not among the leaders as they make the Canal Turn now, it stands very little chance of winning.

The last fence, the thirtieth, is the fourteenth on the first circuit and it presents formidable problems for the comparatively few that reach this point in the race. The psychological strain on the jockey is of course immense. There is said to be a deafening roar from the crowd – a roar which has its place in Grand National lore as a possible cause of Devon Loch's downfall.

There is nearly 500 yards' run-in to the winning-post, and it is during this long run-in, when many horses are exhausted, that the dramas of the National frequently take place.

So much for the fences, but what is it like to face them? Dick Francis says 'Riding for the first time at Liverpool is like crossing the equator' and going over Becher's for the first time he had 'an extensive view of Liverpool for what seemed a very long time'. He goes on, 'I find I cannot properly describe the ecstasy of Aintree: no one who has not ridden there can understand it, and some of those who have, do not feel it. Most of the horses which run there positively enjoy Liverpool.'

Another jockey felt differently. 'Usually the National is more of a worry than a pleasure to anyone riding in it.' The reasons are many – not merely the individual fences, but the way they are sited, and the order in which they are placed, and the effect of one on another. Another factor, related to the size, struck another jockey, who wrote, 'What was so different from normal steeplechase fences was the time it takes to land. There was a noticeable gap between the summit of the fence and the time it took to land.'

Gen. 'Monkey' Blacker, presumably acquainted with the stiff upper lip, has said that 'while inspecting this course before your first ride at Aintree it is hard to keep the conversation going in the lighthearted and cheerful style desirable'.

Christopher Collins describes how he went to Aintree with his horse Mr Jones, bought shortly before the 1965 race. 'I set off to walk the course. I felt a bit white – people told me afterwards I looked ghastly. I walked on round; I didn't really mind what I saw. The fences were big but I could almost look forward to jumping them . . . For years I had fed myself on Aintree literature. The descriptive powers of the writers and my own timidity had built up the fences into shadowy monsters . . . After passing the last I caught up with someone I know; I said that I had not found it as bad as all that. He told me to wait until I saw the Chair. I looked forward towards a dark green bungalow which rose out of a moat.' Collins came third.

Of course to fall at a fence must terrify. Gerry Wilson, who rode Golden Miller in 1934 said, 'There were some thirty-odd horses behind us, and you can imagine what it felt like, crouching down in the ditch, and seeing horses and bellies going over our heads. The noise was terrific as they hit the guard rail.' Some special tension is often the cause of these falls; for example at the first fence, which is not big – 4 ft 6 in. high – but comes after a long run from the starting-gate, and the nerves build up. In 1951 nearly one-third of the field fell at the first fence.

The tension is created from the moment the jockeys arrive at Aintree. Bob Champion describes it as 'at times unbearable. Preliminaries before the race seem to last forever, and in the jockeys' room a curious change in personality affects many of the riders. Men who are usually the life and soul of the party sit silently staring fixedly at the floor.' He says, 'You begin to wonder what the hell you are doing riding in such a race and wish you were hundreds of miles away . . . You are about to tackle the biggest fences in the business and the whole world is waiting to see you make a fool of yourself.'

This from a man who had faced the terrors of cancer . . .

5: Highlights of the National

The word 'steeplechasing' has its origin, according to some sources, in the early part of the nineteenth century on a Leicestershire hunting-field, when, after a fruitless day after the fox, one of the riders suggested a race to the church spire at Melton, which could be seen in the distance. 'What a great day it was without those hounds.' To this day, there is a chase to the steeple at Melton, *in memoriam.* Another source says that two horsemen, drunk or sober, in or out of their wits, fix upon a steeple to which they make a straight cut. A third says that in 1752 Mr O'Callaghan challenged Mr Blake over 4½ miles to the church of St Leger, which had its steeple in view throughout.

1827
A hotelier, Mr Lynn, opened a flat racecourse at Aintree, and this met with general approval as prior to this it was necessary to go to the sands of Mersey or Ormskirk, 15 miles away.

1836
My Lynn introduced a steeplechase at Maghull (some miles from Aintree) called the Grand Liverpool Steeplechase and run 'for gentlemen only'. The winner was The Duke, ridden by the now famous Capt. Becher, the leading professional jockey of his time, whose father had been a horse-dealer. He was not a cavalryman but the Duke of Buckingham gave him the honorary

title of 'Captain'. Some called him 'bumptious and thrusting' although he is said to have been glad to oblige the company with a song even at the end of a bad day.

1837
Another Maghull sweepstake for 25 sovereigns each with 10 sovereigns added. The winner, The Duke, was described as a 'hunting cob'. By this time, Lynn had persuaded the civic authorities to support the race.

1838
The Grand Liverpool Steeplechase continued. It is not to be supposed that Surtees was right when he said 'When it is too bad for anything they called it Grand.' The winner was Sir Henry ridden by Tom Olliver.

1839
William Lynn again organized a race, the first at Aintree, but resigned 'due to indisposition' leaving the organization to the race committee which included two earls (Derby and Sefton), and three lords, Lord George Bentinck (of the Jockey Club), Lord Robert and Lord Stanley Grosvenor. The race was so popular that guests at local hotels slept four in a bed. According to Mirabel Topham this was the first Grand National, but it was called the third Grand Liverpool Steeplechase. It was won by Jem Mason riding Lottery, a horse so highly regarded that race-course executives elsewhere framed their entry conditions 'Open to all horses except Lottery'.

Capt. Becher was leading the field in 1839 when his horse fell at the famous fence which in those days had a brook 6 ft wide. To avoid the oncoming horses, Becher stayed where he had fallen, in the brook, muttering that he never knew water tasted so filthy without brandy. He caught his horse, remounted, but later fell again into more water.

Becher was the leading professional jockey of his time who had held a commission in the Buckinghamshire Yeomanry. He had a thick black beard and slept on horseback or in post-chaises, travelling from one meeting to another. When his fortunes declined he was appointed a sack inspector for Great Northern Railways.

1840

Mr Power, an Irish amateur, was riding a horse Valentine, and bet that he would be first over the Wall fence in front of the stands. At Bechers he was almost a furlong ahead of everything except Lottery. At the ninth, Valentine stopped, reared up on his hind legs and then half-lunged, half-corkscrewed over the fence. They went on to be the first over the Wall and win the bet. The race was won by Jerry, who was bought and sold several times before the race.

By the 1840s, the two fields before Becher's were of wheat, so the original steeplechase course was open country with some man-made fences. For example, the Wall was constructed of stone topped with turf, 5 ft in height.

1841

The race was won by Charity. Third was Peter Simple, but he is believed to be a different horse from that of the same name that won in 1844 and 1853.

1842

Won by Gay Lad, whose owner also owned Lottery.

1843

The race, now a handicap for the first time, was won by Lord Chesterfield's Vanguard.

1844

Discount won, as Tom Tug, the favourite, furnished entertainment by running away and half-scaring his jockey to death.

1845

The National had now caught on. 'On Wednesday last the town of Liverpool was filled by one of the most brilliant companies that ever graced a provincial meeting . . . the grandstand and its enclosure were filled with fashionables.' The race was won by Cure All, a horse described as 'a brute, picked up in Northampton for fifty pounds'.

1846

Pioneer won, much to the amazement of the crowd, as he had

appeared in the paddock with a long shaggy coat and protruding bones. His owner was considerably put out, as he had taken care not to back him.

1847

A journalist invented the name 'Grand National', which has stuck ever since.

Matthew was the first Irish horse with an Irish jockey up to win the National.

1848

Chandler, a horse which at one time pulled a chandler's cart, and was not even given a name, won the race. The rider, Capt. Little, known as 'Captivating Charlie', was only twenty-seven years old.

1849

Won by Peter Simple whose owner and rider, John Cunningham, bought him two days before the race. His rider, Tom Cunningham met Tom Davies, the Cyril Stein of his day, on a railway station, waiting for the Liverpool train. He bet £3,000 to £30 he would win. He did. On the proceeds he got married and set up in France as a trainer. The rider of the horse he beat, Capt. D'Arcy, tried to bribe him to lose as they neared the post.

1850

Abd-el-Kader won in the fastest time then on record, a particularly remarkable feat as he was such a small horse. His mother was discovered when the near-side leader on the Shrewsbury coach.

1851

Abd-el-Kader won again, this time by half a neck. This popular horse was called Little Ab.

1852

The winner, Miss Mowbray, described as 'a rat of a thing', had been a neglected hunter.

1853

Peter Simple won again, beating Miss Mowbray by 3 lengths. He was ridden by Tom Olliver who said 'I was born and bred hopelessly insolvent.'

1854
The two best horses, Abd-el-Kader and Miss Mowbray (who had been got at) were out of the race and Bourton won. His owner then sold him into retirement for £50, but he had to be put down after racing at Warwick.

1855
Won by an Irish stallion, Wanderer, in a hailstorm. Wanderer was believed to be a descendant of the famous Eclipse. The race is usually won by geldings.

1856
Topham was criticized for cutting the size of the fences this year. Free Trader won, ridden by the famous professional jockey, George Stevens, who won on Emblem in 1863 and Emblematic in the following year. Stevens also won on The Colonel in 1869 and 1870.

1857
Emigrant was sold by one trainer to another to cover his losses at cards. A week before the National, Emigrant's jockey injured his arm in a hunting accident, so he rode the race with the arm strapped to his side. He narrowly beat a horse called Weathercock, owned by the very trainer who had sold Emigrant.

1858
The weather was so bad that the National could not be run on the appointed day and was run three days later although the weather was still so poor that only 500 attended. Little Charlie ridden by William Archer won. Archer went to Russia to ride horses for the Tsar. The year before, Archer's son Fred was born, and he became the most famous flat-racing jockey of the second half of the century. He shot himself in a delirium before he was thirty, leaving a fortune.

1859
Again won by an entire horse (a stallion) called, strangely, Half Caste, a six-year-old.

1860

Thomas Pickernell won on Anatis. He used the *nom de course* of Mr Thomas because his family were clerics. Later he won on the famous horse The Lamb.

1861

This race must have been rather dull, as a historian records: 'Nobody was injured seriously, though several riders had narrow escapes.' Jealousy won.

1862

The Huntsman owned by Vicomte de Namur won in a race that was marred by the unfortunate death of the jockey James Wynne, whose horse rolled on him. His father had ridden Matthew to victory.

1863/4

The first major alterations were made in the size of the fences – they were reduced in size. The two sisters, Emblem and Emblematic won, ridden by George Stevens.

1865

A battle royal between two soldiers, a guardsman, Capt. Coventry, riding Alcibiade and Capt. Tempest of 11th Hussars riding Hall Court, the former winning by a head. Although there have been many close races, there has never been a dead heat.

1866

Salamander, the winner, was bought by a Mr Studd from a hovel in Ireland, and he started at 40–1.

1867

A first victory for John Page, a professional jockey of the old school, riding Cortolvin, who won again in 1872 on Casse Tête, a weedy mare.

1868

One of the most famous horses to win the National was The Lamb. The horse was so called because he was very gentle, and a pundit of the day said he was not strong enough to carry a man's boots. In 1870, his rider, Mr George Ede, who rode as 'Mr Edwards' was killed when riding at Aintree, and a new jockey had to be found.

1869/70
The Colonel, ridden by George Stevens, won in both these years, thus becoming the first horse and jockey partnership to win twice. The Colonel was later sold to Germany and it was said that the Emperor of Russia rode him on parade when reviewing his troops on their return from the Franco-Prussian war. His jockey was thrown and killed at Cheltenham in 1871.

The Society for the Prevention of Cruelty to Animals issued a summons against George Holman because of his excessive whipping and spurring of The Doctor during this race.

1871
When The Lamb came to run in the National of 1871 Lord Poulett, his owner, had to find another rider. Some time before the race, his lordship had two dreams. In the first The Lamb finished last, but in the second he won by four lengths and Lord Poulett claimed that he 'saw' not only colours of cerise and blue, but also the jockey wearing them – Mr Tommy Pickernell, who rode as 'Mr Thomas'. The owner wrote to the rider the following day asking him to take the ride and telling him of his two dreams. At Aintree The Lamb started favourite and won easily. The crowd was so enthusiastic that The Lamb lost most of his tail to souvenir hunters, and Lord Poulett lost his gold watch. Ben Lord, a jockey and gambler who had formerly owned The Lamb, heard that The Lamb had been sold. He cut his jugular vein with a razor and one month later the horse fell at Baden Baden and had to be destroyed.

1872
The race was won by Casse Tête, a lucky win in a day full of accidents. She was described as a varmity-looking, washed-out chestnut mare, whose owner, known as Old Boots, bought her for 200 guineas.

1873
Disturbance won, owned by Capt. Machell. The Captain was

one of the most famous and interesting personalities in racing, who retired from the Army and managed a famous stable near Newmarket. 'His cleverness in turning a seemingly mediocre horse into a very good one greatly distressed the touts.' At the banquet at Brigg to honour the jockey the menu admonished 'Disturbance but no row'.

1874
Another Machell winner, Reugny. Reugny, Disturbance and another runner owned by the Captain had been bought for 1,200 guineas, and the Captain sold them for 12,000. But, alas, their new owner made them jump over fancy obstacles for the benefit of a house party with the result that they were ruined for racing.

1875
Pathfinder won, ridden by 'Mr Thomas' (Mr Pickernell). This was his eighteenth National, and he took a little drink to provide 'jumping power'.

1876
Regal won, owned by Capt. Machell. The horse was only five years old. Since 1940 all winners have been eight years old or over. The future Viceroy of India also rode in the race, fell, broke his neck, but fortunately it slipped back into place.

1877
Mr Hobson (who hung on to his saddle when jumping) was one of the few owners to win as a rider – and his horse Austerlitz was a five-year-old. He only rode in this one National.

1878
The Prince of Wales visited Aintree as Sefton's guest. The winner was Shifnal.

1879
All four Beasley brothers rode in this race, won by The Liberator, an outstanding winner who had come second the previous year.

1880
The winner, Empress, stood over 16 hands. Tommy Beasley,

Empress's rider, lost a stirrup during the later part of the race, and in trying to regain it lost a good deal of ground but triumphed in the end by 2 lengths over The Liberator.

1881
Woodbrook won, ridden by Mr T. Beasley in appalling conditions and in the presence of the Empress of Austria. The horse died the following year.

1882
Lord Manners, a serving Guards officer, bought an unsound horse, Seaman, in Ireland for £2,000 and sent him to Newmarket to be trained. On the day of the race it snowed, and the trainer, Capt. Machell, told Lord Manners to tie a knot in his reins and leave the rest to Seaman. Manners won by a head. The horse he beat, Cyrus, was owned by the man who had sold him the dud Seaman. Seaman was broken down and was put into family retirement. Lord Manners rarely rode again. His win was the more remarkable because 'Hoppy' as he was called, although a great rider to hounds, had only ridden one other race under Rules.

1883
The Austrian Prince Charles Kinsky on his mare Zoedone was one of the few owners to win as a rider. His groom is said to have advised him 'Hunt on the first circuit, and then, and not before, start to race.' A contemporary described the horse as the finest jumper in the world and 'the safest conveyance in the race'.

1884
Mr Wilson, an amateur, won two consecutive Nationals and rode in a total of seventeen. This year he was riding Voluptuary, which ended its days on the stage at Drury Lane in a Grand National scene, where the jockey was paid an extra five shillings each night to fall in the water.

1885
Roquefort won, again ridden by Mr Wilson. This was a year of the greatest importance in the development of the course, as it was all grass for the first time, and railed in from start to finish.

1886

Won by Old Joe, the type of horse that makes people say that the National has been won by all sorts of 'queer ones'. He was described as a horse that had done everything except play the fiddle.

1887

Gamecock won.

1888

Playfair won, with Frigate second.

1889

Tommy Beasley won on Frigate after seven attempts by the mare and the brothers. Frigate is said to have been the best mare to have won the National.

1890

Four Grand National winners ran in this race, but Ilex, the favourite beat them all. In the following two years, Ilex came third on each occasion and was then retired to hunt with the Surrey packs. During the 1890s the first tipster to operate at Aintree stood outside a hut and sold envelopes at 3d. each. He was called Liverpool Charlie.

1891

The only objection ever lodged to a National winner – it was disallowed. The horse was Come Away and the jockey Harry Beasley, the grandfather of the 1961 winner.

1892

Captain Roddy Owen was a popular soldier rider who in the previous seven years rode over 250 winners including several for the Royal family. He won easily on Father O'Flynn, but two days later he applied to go abroad and after four years in Egypt, died of cholera. Father O'Flynn went on to come second in the 1896 National.

1893

Cloister won by 40 lengths, breaking several records. 'Cloister first and rest nowhere.' His jockey said to him 'All right Cloister, all right. You know more about 'em than I do, I dare say, so carry on and jump 'em as you like.'

1894
Why Not won at the age of thirteen years. Lord Shaftsbury's Carrollstown, who came sixth, was so exhausted in finishing that he dropped dead in the paddock.

1895
The first appearance of Manifesto who won by 20 lengths in 1897 and won again in 1899. He finished fourth to Wild Man from Borneo.

1896
The Soarer won, with Father O'Flynn second (he had won in 1892).

1897
Manifesto's first victory at the age of nine – he won easily, and won again in 1899. He was one of the best-looking horses ever to win the National and his intelligence matched his looks.

1898
Drogheda won in a snowstorm.

1899
Photography of racing was beginning. Manifesto won again.

1900
King Edward VII's horse Ambush II beat the great Manifesto. 'There were actually tears in men's eyes at the thought of Manifesto's defeat. I can write no more about it; there are some things about which it appears almost sacrilege to write in commonplace black and white,' said a contemporary.

1901
The snow was deep enough to cause protests. Grudon's owner packed his horse's hooves with butter to prevent the snow accumulating, and won in the fast time of 9 minutes 47 seconds.

1902

Shannon Lass was one of the last mares to win the National. Manifesto was third.

1903

Drumcree won by 10 lengths, with Manifesto again third.

1904

The winner, Moifaa, had arrived in England by swimming ashore from a wreck. Manifesto's last National; he was sixteen years of age and finished ninth. In those days you could go by train from London to Aintree and back with food on the train for 48 shillings.

1905

The first horse past the post, Ascetic's Silver, had no rider. But he ran again the following year and won. Kirkland, trained by a clergyman from County Limerick, won the race.

1906

Nearly all the jockeys riding in the race were professionals. The winner, Ascetic's Silver, was owned by Prince Hatzfeldt.

1907

Eremon won. His jockey, Newey, rode all the way from the second fence with only one stirrup.

1908

Rubio won, the first American-bred horse to win the National.

1909

Lutteur III, a French horse, owned by Mr J. Hennessy of brandy fame, won the race.

1910

Jenkinstown, the winner, was bought in strange circumstances. In 1908 James Daley's son met Mr Stanley Howard at Sandown races and said his father had advised him to buy the horse. When Howard said he could not afford it, young Daley said 'My father said that in case you answered like that I was to say "Damn the money. I'll send the horse for you."' And he claimed it would win the National, which it did.

1911
Only one horse, Glenside, completed the course without mishap, due to the appalling weather.

1912
Lester Piggott's grandfather, Ernest, a very strong finisher, won on Jerry M.

1913
Won by Covertcoat, owned by the 1912 winner, Sir C. Assheton-Smith, once described as the worst-tempered man in England.

1914
Sunloch, the winner, began his career in farmers' hurdle races.

1915
Ally Sloper won for Lady Nelson, the first woman owner to win the National. She bought the horse for £700. After this race, the racecourse was requisitioned for the rest of the war.

1916/17/18
Three substitute races were run at Gatwick, which was totally unlike Aintree. But in the 1939–45 war Gatwick was razed to the ground to make an airfield and an underground storage for gas.

1919
Poethlyn, owned by a woman, won for the second time, having been victorious at Gatwick. He was sold as a weakly foal for £17 and bought back as a two-year-old for 50 guineas. The jockey was Ernest Piggott, who had won on Jerry M.

1920
Troytown won and but for a fatal accident in France the following year, he might have proved to be a greater horse than Cloister and Manifesto.

1921

Harry Brown, riding The Bore, broke his collar-bone and re-mounted to finish second. The race was won by Shaun Spadah who was the only horse to remain on his feet throughout the race.

1922

Music Hall, the winner, was ridden by L. B. Rees, his brother Fred having won the previous year. He had been bought for a few hundred pounds.

1923

Sergeant Murphy won, watched by George V who was standing in what Lord Sefton called his private box, a farm-cart positioned at the Canal Turn.

1924

Master Robert, the winner, an ex-plough horse, judged too slow for racing was returned to the farm, then sold for £50. He was found to have a diseased bone and put in the hands of a famous vet by his owner Lord Airlie.

1925

Double Chance, the winner, was given by Mr Anthony de Rothschild to the trainer Frederick Archer 'because the horse was unsound'. Archer hunted him, rested him, sold him and he finally won the National.

1926

Won by Jack Horner who had been bought for 125 guineas in a group of hunters, and re-sold to an American for 4,000 guineas two weeks before the race.

1927

The first radio broadcast of the race by Meyrick Good of *Sporting Life*. Good enthusiastically shouted into the microphone at the end 'Come on Ted – you'll do it!'. Ted Leader was riding Sprig. owned by Mrs Partridge, who was seventy-three years old, and kept Sprig in training in memory of her son who was killed in the war. In many villages near her home, people returning from hunting heard the church bells ringing as all Sprig's winnings were given to charity.

1928

Only two horses finished out of a field of forty-two. The winner, Tipperary Tim, who won at 100–1, had been sold for £50 as a yearling. Easter Hero created havoc by running up and down the open ditch at the Canal Turn and putting thirty-five of the forty-one runners out of the race. Before the year was out, his owner, Capt. Albert Lowerstein the financier, had flung himself out of his private plane to his death over the English Channel. Easter Hero was eventually bought by Jack Whitney, the millionaire American owner.

1929

Gregalach won, in a field of sixty-six starters, beating Easter Hero, who should have won a National, but never did.

1930

The winner, Shaun Goilin, was sold as a three-year-old for 55 guineas. In the war, his jockey was serving in the army, got depressed, and blew his brains out with a rifle.

1931

Grackle won in a very fast time. For the first time the National ceased to be an 'open' race in which any horse could compete, and it was now necessary to 'qualify' as to age, weight and racing record. Despite this, eighty-five horses were entered and forty-three started. The 1931 Grand National was the first steeplechase on which the Irish Sweep was held. The Sweep had been legalized in 1930 as the Irish Hospital Sweepstakes. The winning ticket in 1931 paid out £354,724. The Italian owner of a café in Battersea had bought it but sold it for £10,000 before the race was run.

1932

In *Aintree Iron* Fred Rimmell wrote: 'I rode a horse called Provocative in the Grand National and was offered £100 if he finished. He was lame going to the post, and [a leading writer] said "Well if I were you I'd settle for the first £100 and let him come under starters' orders and pull him up after he's jumped the first fence."' Rimmell couldn't pull him up and 'he finished up lame, but all the connections were delighted because of their bet that he would complete the course. In those days they used to bet against any horse finishing the course. The fences were bigger, straighter and nothing like as inviting as they are today.' The winner trained by T. Rimmell was Forbra, a reject from flat racing, owned by a bookmaker.

1933
Kellsboro' Jack, who won in the record time of 9 minutes 28 seconds, was bought by F. Ambrose Clark, one of the heirs to the Singer Sewing Machine fortune, who thought himself unlucky with horses, and so sold the horse to his wife for £1. Kellsboro Jack is buried in the USA.

1934
This was the year of Dorothy Paget and Golden Miller. She acquired the horse in payment of a gambling debt from Basil Briscoe, who stipulated that he should train it. Golden Miller was called 'The horse of the century'.

1935
Gerry Wilson, the jockey riding Golden Miller reported that he had been offered £3,000 to stop the horse. He fell, and Dorothy Paget, in a temper, sacked the jockey and removed her horse from Basil Briscoe's stable. Although the horse had a reputation for hating Aintree, Dorothy Paget unsuccessfully entered him again both in 1936 and 1937. Briscoe never got going afterwards, soon gave up his licence, peddled dung and, widowed and sick, finally died a broken man in 1951, although Golden Miller lived another six years. Reynoldstown, called after his Irish home, was the winner.

1936
Riding Davy Jones, the Hon. Anthony Mildmay lying second at the second-to-last fence had decided against tying his reins in the knot which every rider does to avoid putting two much strain on the buckle. As the pin of the buckle shot past the bar, the reins flew out of the rider's hands and the horse, with no indication as to direction coming from its helples rider, ran out before the last fence, leaving Reynoldstown to win his second successive National. Reynoldstown was ridden by Fulke Walwyn.

1937

Royal Mail, a black horse, won. The majority of winners have been bay, brown or chestnut.

1938

The du Pont heiress, Marion du Pont, who married the film star Randolph Scott, had sent over from America the famous horse Battleship, which had won the American Grand National in 1934. Battleship won after a thrilling race, but it was so close that the judge had to decide. The odds were 40–1.

1939

Workman won by three lengths. He was an Irish horse and Dublin was said to have put its shirt on him.

1940

Bogskar won. But his jockey Flt.-Sergeant M. A. Jones, a professional rider, was killed two years later flying a Spitfire.

1941/5

The racecourse housed 16,000 troops, mainly Americans, and was used as a depot for trucks. The Tophams, from their house, guarded the Grand National circuit jealously throughout the war. There was no racing.

1946

First Grand National after the war. Bobby Petre, a captain in the Scots Guards, was twenty lengths behind at the second-to-last fence, but went on to win on Lovely Cottage. A crowd of 400,000 watched.

1947

The Labour Government requested that the race be moved from Friday to Saturday, presumably to improve productivity. Eddie Dempsey, the winning jockey on Caughoo, was involved in a fist fight followed by a lawsuit, when his assailant claimed that he had taken his horse through the mist and across the plough after jumping the fence before Becher's on the final circuit, rejoining the course at the fence after Valentines, thereby missing twenty of the thirty fences. The magistrates found for Dempsey, who had won by 20 lengths. His odds were 100–1.

1948

Eddie Reavey, riding First of the Dandies, got a wrong impression of the route to be taken, and missed out the last jump. So the winner was Sheila's Cottage, a mare, owned by a Grimsby trawlerman who started life as a half-crown-a-week errand boy. The first mare to win since 1902, Sheila's Cottage's trainer described her as an 'ornery old cow' and 'a good, game plodder'. Lord Mildmay, riding Cromwell, failed to win.

1949

Lord Mildmay failed to win the National again. The owner of the winner, Russian Hero, had £10 on his horse at 300–1.

1950

Freebooter won, and to everyone's dismay, Lord Mildmay on Cromwell lost again. Later in the year he drowned off the Devon coast, probably due to cramp. During this decade, the swinging fifties, the race was always a time of huge parties at the Adelphi Hotel where the chief sufferers were the chandeliers. However, there were other sufferers and the knowing ones remembered not to put their shoes outside their doors. One year the shoes from eighty-four rooms were thrown out of the window on to the pavement below.

1951

Won by Nickel Coin who was bought for 50 guineas, but subsequently sold, and the owner's son bought her back with his gratuity. The jockey was an ex-paratrooper and prisoner-of-war, Johnny Bullock. The starter made a hash of things and ten horses fell at the first fence.

1952

Mrs Topham's disaster when she banned the BBC and put in her own commentators, one of whom said the winner, Teal, had fallen at the first fence. He had once been offered for sale at £2 10s. 0d. with no takers in Ireland, and changed hands in England at 35 guineas.

1953

The winner, Early Mist, was owned by a young Dublin businessman who danced a victory jig in the unsaddling enclosure to cries of 'Well done Mincemeat Joe.'

1954
Won by Royal Tan, also owned by Mincemeat Joe. His business started to go to pieces in 1954 and on the eve of the National there was a row when he had a money quarrel with his jockey in the Adelphi Hotel. The trainer of both horses was the famous Irishman Vincent O'Brien.

1955
The course was waterlogged so the water jump was omitted. The winner was Quare Times, a brilliant jumper but an unsound horse, again trained by Vincent O'Brien.

1956
The famous year in which the Queen Mother's horse, Devon Loch, ridden by Dick Francis, fell when in the lead about 50 yards from the finishing post. No explanation of the horse's strange behaviour has ever been found. He could not go on, and the race was won by ESB.

1957
Sundew had already failed twice, and his owner tried to sell him for £3,500. She could not do so; he was ridden by Fred Winter, who achieved his first National win.

1958
Mr What won, but although he later entered another thirty steeplechases, he never won another.

1959
Oxo, an ex-point-to-pointer, won.

1960
The story of the winner goes back to one day in 1949 when the Marquis of Linlithgow was having breakfast with his family at the family estate of Hopetown, Midlothian. Looking up from *The Times*, he said to his astonished children 'Poor as I am, it is beyond my means to aspire to breeding a Derby winner, but it

would give me the greatest satisfaction to breed a Grand National winner here at Hopetown.' Poor is relative, is it not, if you have been Viceroy of India? His daughter recounted how she nearly spilled her porridge.

Within a week a friend offered to give him a young half-bred mare which was too hot to handle 'for the cost of the transport'. Linlithgow's daughter hunted her for one season and then retired her for breeding. The Marquis died in 1952. His daughter married a Gore-Langton, a well-known horsey family, and became an MFH, and the family sold one of the horse's offspring, Merryman II, to a member of the hunt, Miss Wallace, who hunted and point-to-pointed the horse. He eventually won by 15 lengths, and went on to finish second in 1961.

1961
This was the year chosen by the Russians to send over their three best chasers to challenge for the Grand National. They were doomed from the start, and ended in humiliation. The race was won by Nicolaus Silver, the first grey to win since The Lamb. The jockey was the grandson of the 1891 winner Harry Beasley.

1962
Fred Winter won on Kilmore, his second National win. Later he had two winners as trainer. This year the fences were sloped on the take-off side to make the going easier.

1963
Teasy Weasy Raymond the hairdresser won with Ayala at 66–1. The jockey was Pat Buckley, only nineteen, and he narrowly beat John Lawrence (now Lord Oaksey the journalist). The trainer was Keith Piggott, father of Lester.

1964
Team Spirit, owned by three Americans, was the first US-owned winner since Battleship in 1938.

1965
Jay Trump won, the first victory for a horse ridden by an American, Tommy Smith. He was trained by Fred Winter.

1966

The race was won by Anglo. He was sold for 110 guineas to a farmer by the late Gen. Randle Fielden who became Senior Steward of the Jockey Club. 'Even pundits on racing are sometimes made to look foolish,' said Clive Graham.

1967

During the race, a loose horse running down the fence caused trouble at the twenty-third. With one exception, all the horses were brought to a halt. The exception was Foinavon, a moderate horse, who won by an official 15 lengths. His jockey, John Buckingham, was riding his first National.

1968

The winner, Red Alligator, was half brother to the 1966 winner Anglo, and was bought at the Dublin sales for only 70 guineas.

1969

The winning owner, the American Thomas H. McCoy Jnr, heard the news by letter. His horse, Highland Wedding, had raced in 1966 and 1968. The jockey, Dubliner Eddie Harty, was riding in shows when he was six years old.

1970

Won by Gay Trip, trained by Fred Rimmell; it was his third National winner and in 1976 he went on to have a fourth with Rag Trade.

1971

Won by Specify. One of the most exciting Nationals on record with five horses together at the last fence.

1972

Well to Do won. Mrs Heather Sumner, of a famous Oxfordshire sporting family, bought him for £750 in 1966. But she died of cancer in 1971 and left him to her trainer, Tim Forster, in her will. The horse was only entered for the National half an hour before nominations closed. He was related to three of the greatest Grand National winners of all time – Gregalach, Reynoldstown and Royal Mail – and one of the unluckiest losers, Easter Hero.

1973

Red Rum is the legendary horse which won three Nationals, yet was stabled behind a Southport car showroom. With one fence to go, he was 15 lengths behind the favourite, Crisp, but caught him and won in the record time of 9 minutes 1.9 seconds. His owner was in his eighties. This was the year in which Mrs Topham sold Aintree to Bill Davies.

1974

Red Rum won carrying 12 stone. The race was organized by Bill Davies, the new owner of Aintree, but only a few thousand people attended, due to his increased entrance charges.

1975

L'Escargot beat Red Rum by 15 lengths. The race was again run by Bill Davies, but the following year he handed over to Ladbrokes.

1976

Won by Rag Trade, Teasy Weasy Raymond's second winner. Ladbrokes took a lease on the race and organized it for the next seven years.

1977

No horse before had ever won three Nationals, and Red Rum did so by 25 lengths. His jockey was Tommy Stack who led over the last mile. This year was notable also in that the first woman rode in the National, Charlotte Brew.

1978

Lucius won. The nearest a woman trainer had got to having a National winner (until 1983) was when the Irish Peggy St John Nolan's horse Drumroan just failed to catch Lucius. Incidentally, since the war Irish trainers have saddled only six winners of the race, three by Vincent O'Brien, though it has been dominated by Irish-bred horses.

1979

Rubstic was a Scottish horse and it is rare indeed for the Scots to be mentioned in the context of the Grand National.

1980

Ben Nevis, the winner, an English horse bought by an American over the dinner-table after a shooting-party in Yorkshire, and ridden by his son-in-law Charles Fenwick, had come a cropper in 1979. Charlie, an American banker, spent several weeks in England in the early part of 1980, and this paid off. Only four horses finished. An indication of American enthusiasm for Aintree was the owner's comment, 'The whole of fox-hunting America would rather win your Grand National than any other race.'

1981

A magnificent race by Bob Champion, who was fighting cancer, and his horse Aldaniti who had had tendon trouble. They won by 4 lengths.

1982

Geraldine Rees became the first woman to complete the National course. The winner was Grittar, ridden by Dick Saunders, the oldest man ever to win the National.

1983

Mrs Jenny Pitman created racing history when she became the first woman to train a winner, the eight-year-old Corbiere. The owner was a twenty-two-year-old, having acquired the horse from his father, Alan Burrough, the gin maker, who in turn had created racing history after the war by winning the Silver Goblets at Henley having had one leg amputated.

6: Heroes and Heroines

In 1907, G. Finch Mason wrote a book entitled *Heroes and Heroines of the Grand National*. Strangely enough his book is not about heroes specifically, and certainly not about heroines, unless you count stallions and mares, and there are not many of those since it is mainly geldings who enter the National. Heroines, in any case, were not much in evidence in the world of the National, as it was essentially a man's world in 1907 and before, or, as Finch Mason put it in his author's preface, a world of 'noblemen and gentlemen'.

Therefore it seems timely, nearly eighty years having passed since Finch Mason, to try to pick out the heroes and heroines who made the race what it is. Such a selection cannot be fair of course, since it may well be said that everyone who enters the Grand National is a hero or a heroine. So let it be admitted that this selection is arbitrary, and does not duplicate those who are dealt with in more detail elsewhere in the book.

1837
William Lynn, the man who started it all, was not so much a hero as an enthusiast who sparked off a fire and kept it alive with the help of Lord Sefton or Lord Dashalong as he was called. When the race moved to Aintree in 1839 there was however something heroic, and certainly tragic, about the way he resigned from the

management of the race, leaving it to the aristocracy to take charge, and fading away to die almost destitute.

1839
Jem Mason had a strong, perhaps heroic, element in his nature and it was said the famous horse Lottery hated him and had to be tricked into allowing him into the saddle. Perhaps it was because Mason always raced in white kid gloves, and had his clothes made for him free by a tailor in Savile Row.

1856
You would have to be a hero to win the race five times, once in 1856, then in two consecutive years, and again in two consecutive years. But that is what that tough Cheltenham professional George Stevens did. He won on Freetrader in 1856, on Emblem in 1863 and again the following year on Emblematic (this being the first time a jockey had won in two consecutive years). In 1869 and 1870 he achieved the double again on The Colonel. He met a strange death when his horse was taking him home after a party in a pub. Stevens's hat was blown off, his horse bolted and he was thrown to the ground with fatal consequences.

1870
Tom Scott jumped the course, horseless, for a bet. A 'very athletic' officer in the Royal Artillery later did the same thing. They were both heroes although not National heroes.

1878
The involvement of the Irish in the National goes back to its earliest days, and many of them have been heroes. Take the Beasleys.

In 1878 Tommy Beasley rode for the first time in the National and came second. He was one of five brothers, four of whom rode in the National and only one failed to win a place.

	First	Second	Third
Tommy	1880, 1881, 1889	1878, 1882	1879
Harry	1891	1884, 1885, 1886	1883
Willy		1888	

In 1879 the Irish horse Liberator won, and this was the start of several years of Irish dominance at Aintree, with the Beasley brothers at their peak. Many of the horses came from the most famous stables in Europe, Mr Linde's near the Curragh.

The decade ended with Tommy Beasley winning at Aintree on Frigate.

The following years saw many famous Irish winners. Among the heroic owners were the Widger brothers, who bought Wild Man from Borneo for £600 and won the National in 1895. Another Widger horse, Jerry M, was trained by the Dublin-born Robert Gore (later Sir Charles Assheton-Smith Bt).

More famous Irish horses won into the 1920s, and in 1924 the seventy-four-year-old Harry Beasley rode in the National, completing the course.

1882

A young Guards officer, Lord Manners, who had only ridden in one National Hunt race, bought Seaman for £2,000. As he was so inexperienced, his trainer advised him to let the horse take him over the course (which was smothered in a blinding snowstorm) and at the post he inched his way to lead the famous jockey Tommy Beasley, who had won three Nationals, by a head. Lord Manners's hands were raw and the horse was so broken down that he never ran again. Nor did Lord Manners ever enter for another major race.

1883

Austrian Count Charles Kinsky, later a prince, won on Zoedone, which he had bought for 800 guineas, with 200 guineas more to be paid if the mare won the National. Naturally the Count was keen to win another race, and so join the select band of heroes who have won in consecutive years. Alas, in 1884 he failed. In the following year the Count tried again, after being warned by an anonymous letter that the mare was to be got at. A contemporary account says that detectives guarded her day and night, but as the Count got into the saddle on the day of the race he noticed a spot of blood on the white sleeve of his jacket, against which Zoedone had rubbed her nuzzle. Investigating, he found a minute puncture near her nostril. As many of his friends were 'on the mare' he decided to continue but what followed was the most uncomfortable ride of his life. On the way to the start Zoedone threw him, but he managed to remount and reach the post. When the flag fell the mare rolled about as if she were drunk. Eventually reaching Becher's she fell heavily and lay on her side for about a quarter of an hour. Fortunately the Count was not hurt, despite 'a fine exhibition of courage on his part'. It was surmised that some scoundrel managed to inject the mare with a poison (hartshorn it was thought) by means of a small syringe. Zoedone was never the same mare again, and was useless at stud.

1890
This was almost the last National in which the celebrated Capt. Machell entered a horse, but regrettably it did not finish the course. His first win had been Disturbance in 1873 but he had entered a horse almost every year since 1864, winning in 1873, 1874 and 1876 and being placed several times. After a gap of ten years, he again entered a horse, Chit Chat, in the 1901 race, which was run in a snowstorm.

1908
Rubio coupled with the name of Maj. Douglas-Pennant. The Major bought this horse (from America) for 15 guineas and he won three races before he broke down. The Major then lent him to the landlord of the Prospect Arms at Towcester to pull the station omnibus in the hope that road work would make his legs sound again. Three years later the Major put him back into training and in 1908 Rubio won the National.

1924
Bob Trudgill had had many bad falls and the day before the 1924 National he fell badly again. However, he was determined to win on Master Robert, and did so the next day by three lengths, later collapsing in the weighing room.

1934
The Hon. Dorothy Pagett was an extraordinary character who was expelled from five girls' schools before being sent off to Paris to 'finish'. She lived at Leeds Castle in Kent and derived her fortune from her Whitney-born mother. She tried to make money at motor-racing and then turned to horses. She acquired

Golden Miller from Basil Briscoe, an Australian heir, after one of Sir Melville Ward's chemin de fer parties where he gambled with the likes of Lord Harewood, Jimmy de Rothschild, Alfred Butt and Dorothy. He sold Dorothy the horse after heavy losses, provided she would let him train it.

Clive Graham, the famous commentator, wrote that plump, plain-faced Dorothy Pagett, an eccentric twenty-eight-year-old millionairess, looked as near as she ever became to being radiant as she walked the winner (Golden Miller) on the arm of her frail old father, Lord Queenborough, who it is said won £1,000 on the race. Celebrations were, as always in the 1930s, held at the Adelphi Hotel. The winning owner had a reserved place in the centre of the horseshoe-shaped table on a stage overlooking the band and ballroom. Soon after 8 o'clock the waiters began attending to the 500 guests at £5 a head. The band was under a Mr Joe Orlando. After midnight, Lord Queenborough, who clearly thought his daughter a heroine, arose to propose the toast, 'My daughter, her horse Golden Miller – and the British Empire'.

1936
Reynoldstown, who had won in 1935, was ridden by Fulke Walwyn when victorious for the second time. Although he rode in the National three times, he completed the course only once. Nearly fifty years later, Walwyn, who in the intervening period had trained two National winners and trained for the Queen Mother and Dorothy Paget, was the hero of a special Grand National Day at Ascot. He helped raise £20,000 for the Appeal.

1938
Bruce Hobbs, on Battleship, was the youngest rider ever to win the National, aged seventeen. Mrs Scott, who was a du Pont, bought Battleship who was sent to be trained with Reg Hobbs at Lambourn. His son Bruce won by a matter of inches from the big Irish horse Royal Danieli. The owner was too excited to lead the horse in.

1948
Capt. Neville Crump trained three Grand National winners – Sheila's Cottage, Teal and Merryman II. He is famous for the

heroic words, as he struck Sheila's Cottage on the rump, 'Well done, you old bitch. Make no mistake, she was an absolute swine, a real old brute. She'd bite and kick anybody but she knew what she was about on the racecourse.'

1952

Duque de Alburquerque, a Spaniard of ancient lineage, saw a film of the National when he was eight years of age and was determined to win the race, which he never did. His first attempt was in 1952, on a horse trained by Peter Cazalet. The Duque fell and suffered a cracked vertebra. Ten years later he bought an Irish horse, which had been favourite in 1961. In 1963, with the Duque riding, the horse fell at the twenty-first. In 1965, his horse fell at the ninth, and the Duque suffered a broken leg. The following year his horse stopped at the twenty-sixth. Some years, and many fractures later, he tried again, but his bridle broke. By this time the bookmakers were offering 66–1 against his completing the course. By 1974 they offered 500–1 against his taking part. He was fifty-six years old, and far from fit when he completed the course and finished eighth, despite having broken a collar-bone a week before the race. In 1975, just before the race, he again broke a leg, but almost rode despite his injury, until Fred Winter dissuaded him. The following year he fell very badly at the thirteenth and many horses rode over his body. It was two days before he recovered consciousness. He wanted to return to ride a Spanish horse but mercifully the Jockey Club banned him by introducing a medical examination. So the Duque had to watch the race from Fred Winter's box.

For bravery and perseverence, few can match the Duque.

1955

One of the most famous of trainers was Vincent O'Brien, son of a trainer and breeder, who rode his first winner in 1940. He started by selling a greyhound for £4 and used the money to back a horse he was training, winning at 10–1. He set up a major racing establishment in the Tipperary town of Cashel with the object of winning the National and in 1953 he did so, as well as the Cheltenham Gold Cup and the Irish Derby. In the following year, he entered Royal Tan, who won by a neck. Then, in 1955, Vincent entered Quare Times who won by 12 lengths, despite terrible weather which put the course under water. Ireland turned out to give O'Brien a hero's welcome. Quare Times was paraded through Dublin, bonfires were lit, and the Rock of Cashel illuminated as the winning pair returned home. Between 1948 and 1955 O'Brien thrice won the National, the Cheltenham Gold Cup four times, and the Champion Hurdles three times. He then turned his attention to flat racing with similar success.

1956

Dick Francis is a non-winning hero of the National, who should have won the race if ever this can be said. The tragedy of not winning came about in his eighth National, when 56 yards from the winning-post, out in front on the Queen Mother's Devon Loch, the horse collapsed – rather like someone doing the splits.

Francis was a distinguished jockey whose one ambition had always been to win the National. He had been flying in the Royal Air Force and in 1946 took up amateur racing and became a professional in 1949, riding in the Grand National that year and coming second.

Dick Francis's theory about Devon Loch's collapse is that the tremendous noise of the applause for the Queen Mother's horse as he jumped the last fence, and which grew louder every second, was desperately frightening to the animal, although exhilarating to Francis, and the horse reacted to it by trying to jerk away, breaking the rhythm of his stride and bringing him down.

Francis himself has always been quite philosophical about the 1956 incident, and the Queen Mother said resignedly 'That's racing I suppose.' Francis recounts that she later asked him to Windsor Castle. 'She received me in a sunny room overlooking the mile-long tree-bordered drive which stretches away into Windsor Great Park [where] we talked of the excitement and the heartache.'

Lord Abergavenny advised Francis to hang up his boots, advice he took, and today he is known worldwide as a novelist.

1962

Fred Winter, having won on Sundew in 1957 won again on Kilmore five years later. They said there could be no more popular winner than Winter, who had a formidable steeple-chasing record with 4,000 rides in the period 1947 to 1964 and 313 falls. His father had been a first-class flat-racing jockey, and Fred began as one, but became too heavy. During the war he was a parachutist, and returned to take up National Hunt racing. He hunted and took every opportunity of jumping but had no sooner begun to make his name than he fell badly, broke his leg, and was out of the saddle for a whole season. He was not the ideal build for a good rider over fences – short in leg and stature, but he triumphed by winning the National twice, and, when he became a trainer by fielding two winners, Jay Trump in 1965 and Anglo in 1966.

1967

John Buckingham, twenty-eight years old, riding for the first time in the National, won on Foinaven, a 100–1 outsider, neither his owner nor trainer having bothered to go to the race. Buckingham was only offered the ride on the Wednesday and had to sleep on an armchair on the Friday night before the race, as accommodation hadn't been arranged. At the fence after Becher's, two loose horses ran up and down and destroyed the field. Foinavon had not won a race that season, but Buckingham went on to win by fifteen lengths. Originally Foinavon had been rejected by Anne, Duchess of Westminster, and one of the joint purchasers gave his half-share away, saying that he had wanted to sell it, but there were no takers. The new owners won over £10,000 in bets. The bookies were delighted.

1968

The American grandfather and retired stockbroker Tim Durant, riding in his third Grand National at the age of sixty-eight, fell at Becher's on the second time round. He remounted and completed the course to win a £500 bet which he gave to the Injured Jockeys' Fund.

1972

Mrs Heather Sumner was seriously ill with cancer and in hospital, when she was visited by her trainer Jim Forster. She told him she was convinced Well to Do should run in the National. In her will, she left Jim the choice of her five horses and he chose Well to Do, which was Mrs Sumner's favourite horse. In just another year she would have seen him win the National. Forster was the first owner-trainer to win for nearly forty years and he also won again as a trainer with Ben Nevis ridden by Charlie Fenwick.

1973

Ginger McCain, forever coupled with the name of Red Rum, lived in Lancashire, and kept a modest string of horses in stables at the back of his car showrooms at Southport which enabled him to train his horses on the sands. He had started training in 1969, with a boyhood ambition to win the National. Red Rum came to him in 1972, having been bought at the very high price, for Ginger, of 6,000 guineas. He began racing as a two-year-old and won his first five races. His owner, Mr le Mare, who was in his eighties said, 'I have had three aims ever since I was a young man: to marry a beautiful girl; to become a millionaire and to win the Grand National. Now I have achieved them all and it has made my life.' Red Rum was entered for the 1973 National and with one fence to go Crisp, the favourite, was 15 lengths ahead of him, but Red Rum caught him, to win by three-quarters of a length. He won again in 1974. Finally, in 1977, he did what no horse had ever done before – he won a third National, at the most extraordinary distance of 25 lengths. His jockey said 'Nothing can do justice to this horse, nothing I can say and nothing anyone can write; he is just beyond belief.'

1976

Riding in a lesser race over the course in 1976, John Thorne completed the course, to all intents, bareback. Lord Oaksey said 'Imagine riding bareback over even one fence at Aintree.' Sadly Thorne was killed at a point-to-point in 1982, having ridden in the National several times.

1977

Charlotte Brew became the first woman to ride in the Grand National. She had wanted to do so ever since she had seen Elizabeth Taylor in *National Velvet*. Ladbrokes offered her 500–1 if she could complete the course, but the odds had fallen to 8–1 on the day of the race. She was out dancing until 2 a.m. on the morning of the National. Alas her horse refused at the big open ditch, four from the finish.

1981

Fighting a dreadful battle against cancer, Bob Champion was sustained by the thought of recovering and riding Aldaniti in the Grand National. The horse's trainer, Josh Gifford, who had been told in 1979 that Champion had cancer, thought he could never ride again. By a strange coincidence, Aldaniti was also an invalid with tendon problems. Champion felt that he and Aldaniti had to recover together.

It was Nick Embericos who decided to put Aldaniti back into training for the National. He also backed the horse at 66–1.

On the day of the National, Champion said, 'I badly want to win the race for so many people, in particular the doctors and nurses who kept me going when all hope seemed gone. I also want to win for Josh [Gifford] who kept my job waiting for me and then helped me through a bad patch when my confidence was rock bottom . . . Most of all, I want to win the Grand National for all the patients still in hospital. If any success I have can give people fresh heart and just a bit of hope then everything that has happened to me in the past twenty months will have been worth while.'

They were second favourites at 10–1. Champion wrote 'he was like a cat, so fast, so sure and loving every minute of it'. But by the final run in 'he was so tired but he still had the strength to keep his stride unbroken'.

He won by 4 lengths over John Thorne.

1982

Geraldine Rees became the first woman to complete the National course. She was eighth. The daughter of a trainer, she represented Britain in the Junior Championships in 1973 and competed at Badminton. She failed to buy the horse she wanted to ride in the National but the new owner offered it to her – the horse was Cheers. She was criticized for going so hard for the finish. 'It was shameful the way she forced her exhausted mount to the finishing-line to satisfy her lust for glory,' said one letter.

1982

Dick Saunders retired after winning. He was the first member of the Jockey Club ever to win (he had been elected a year earlier), the oldest man ever to win, and one of two (the other being Lord

John Manners) to win riding only once in the race.

Dick was a true amateur, a Northamptonshire farmer, who had ridden in a great many steeplechases and point-to-points and had done plenty of hunting. He won on Grittar, the favourite, with only seven other horses finishing.

PART TWO
The Pull – and the People

7: The Pull of the National

There are three main reasons why the Grand National attracts the vast interest that it does and why, although the crowds at Aintree itself have now fallen off, the television audience is bigger than ever. No other race attracts so many: far more than the Derby, and international in scope.

The first of the reasons is that the race and everything connected with it has a strange dreamlike quality, so that we expect the unexpected, the illogical, the unreal. Indeed, large numbers of people dream about the National and see the winner in their sleep before the race takes place. A second reason is the forbidden attraction of the cruel, almost tragic element in the race, with the wild riderless horses jumping the fences, and the large group of riders who do not finish.

The third reason is the belief that the race can be won by a horse which is a 'nobody' and that any one of us could find such a horse, which however unlikely would turn out to be the hero of the Grand National.

Why has a story about the Grand National, published first in 1935, and later made into a film, been so extraordinarily popular: *National Velvet* by Enid Bagnold, had rave reviews from the start. Hugh Walpole (highly thought of in his day, if not now) said 'Miss Bagnold has something that belongs to genius,' and Katherine Mansfield (still highly regarded) said 'she could find in all things a grain of living beauty'.

Miss Bagnold came from a socially distinguished family, the daughter of a colonel, and was educated at an exclusive school for girls. In 1920 she married Sir Roderick Jones, KBE. So she could well be expected to deal with the social aspects of horse-racing in general and the Grand National in particular. The social aspects are a significant part of the story she wrote.

National Velvet is about a fourteen-year-old girl Velvet, with a passion for horses, who obtains in a shilling raffle a piebald gelding, with which she wins the Grand National, owner up. At that time it was not permitted for ladies, let alone unlicensed fourteen-year-old girls, to ride under the Rules of Racing. When she thinks of the horse, she immediately says 'I might ride him in the Grand National myself.' She thinks in poetical terms: 'The gorgeous names of horses were cried from mouth to mouth and circulated in a stream of fame: Lottery, The Hermit, the great mare Sceptre; the glorious ancestress Pocohontas, whose blood ran down like Time into her flying children; Easter Hero and The Lamb, that pony stallion.' Grand stuff.

Velvet is aided in her scheme by a man, Mi Taylor, who helped her father, a butcher. Mi had 'been a flyweight boxer, killed his man, because the wretched creature was in status lymphaticus, got exonerated and yet somehow disqualified, tramped the country, held horses, cleaned stables, and drifted nearer and nearer to the racing world, till he knew all about it except the feel of a horse's back'.

Assisted by Mi, Velvet writes to Weatherby's to ask for the rules of entering for the Grand National race. When she enters, her mother provides the entrance fee in sovereigns, and Mi personally takes these to Weatherby's in Cavendish Square.

The night before the race, Velvet is taken by Mi to Liverpool, and she stays at the Adelphi and is told something about the course. Here is more social comment as the taxi took them 'through the mean streets for twenty minutes. It seemed impossible that so great a racecourse could lie buried in so mean a place. Suddenly there was a clearing on the right and the gates. Like the clearing and the gate of a cemetery lifting in the surf of a metropolis.' You may well ask what all that means, but it is clear that Liverpool is non-U, even if the race is acceptable.

Then the race itself.

'At the post the twenty horses were swaying like the sea.

Forward . . . No good! Back again. Forward . . . No good! Back again.

'The line formed . . . and rebroke. Waves of the sea. Drawing a breath . . . breaking. Velvet fifth from the rail, between a bay and a brown. The starter had long finished his instructions. Nothing more was said aloud, but low oaths flew, the cursing and grumbling flashed like a storm. An eye glanced at her with a look of hate. The breaking of movement was too close to movement to be borne. It was like water clinging to the tilted rim of the glass, like the sound of the dreaded explosion after the great shell has fallen. The will to surge forward overlaid by something delicate and terrible and strong, human obedience at bursting point, but not broken. Horses' eyes gleamed openly, men's eyes set like chips of steel. Rough man, checked in violence, barely master of himself, barely master of his horse. The Piebald ominously quiet, and nothing coming from up . . . up went the tape . . .

'The green course poured in a river before her as she lay forward, and with the plunge of movement sat in the stream.

'He heard the thunder coming. It roared up on the wet turn like the single approach of a multiple-footed animal. There were stifled exclamations, grunts, thuds. Something in the air flashed and descended. The first over Becher's! A roar went up from the crowd, then silence. The things flashing in the air were indistinguishable. The tip of a cap exposed for the briefest of seconds. The race went by like an express train, and was gone. Could Velvet be alive in that?

'There was a struggle going on at Becher's; a horse had fallen and was being got over with ropes.

'There was a shout and a horse, not riderless, but ridden by a tugging cursing man, came galloping back through the curling fumes of the mist, rolled its wild eye at the wrong side of Becher's and disappeared away out of the course. An uproar began along the fringes of the crowd. Two more horses came back out of the mist, one riderless. The shades of others could be discerned in the fog. Curses rapped out from unseen mouths.

'Nineteen horses had streamed down to the Canal Turn, and suddenly there across the course, at the boundary of the fog, four horses appeared beyond Valentine's, and among them, fourth, was Velvet's horse, The Piebald.

'The scene immediately before them occupied all the attention. Horses that had fallen galloped by riderless, stirrups flying from their saddles, jockeys returned on foot, covered with mud, limping, holding their sides, some running slowly and miserably over the soggy course, trying to catch and sort the horses.

'He came up to the gates of Melling Road, crossed the road on the fringe of the tan, and suddenly, out of the mist, The Piebald galloped riderless, lolloping unsteadily along, reins hanging, stirrups dangling.'

Although she has won, there is a problem when she falls off the horse and then, to their horror, the officials discover that Velvet is a girl. The matter will have to be referred to Weatherby's and to the National Hunt Committee.

The Press say 'For a woman to complete the National course is regarded as one of the most extraordinary feats in the annals of British racing.'

When Velvet appears before the stewards of the National Hunt Committee (now merged with the Jockey Club) they are a distinguished company described as 'mainly robust and kindly men'. The chairman allows that he only reads *The Times*, and Lord Tunmarch says that the evening papers are 'for the servants' hall'. Velvet tells them she entered because 'the horse jumps lovely and I wanted him to be famous'. They also interview Mi Taylor, who they call 'Taylor' just as they would today.

The National Hunt Committee decide to drop the whole thing because Velvet is a national hero. 'And now, finished with that puzzling mixture of insane intimacy and isolation which is notoriety [concludes Miss Bagnold] Velvet was able to get on quickly to her next adventures. For obviously she was a person to whom things happen.'

The themes of the story then are these:

A nobody becomes famous overnight, but then returns to normal life.

She becomes famous by entering a Grand event, which is organized by Grand people and she becomes – momentarily – Grand.

Accidents of all kinds are a feature of the event, an essential feature, and the heroes of the race are, one might say, accident-prone.

Captain Becher, the most famous of
Grand National riders

Captain Machell, the most successful
of Grand National trainers

Lottery, winner in 1839, seemed to jump as if from a springboard and learned
how to do it with the staghounds

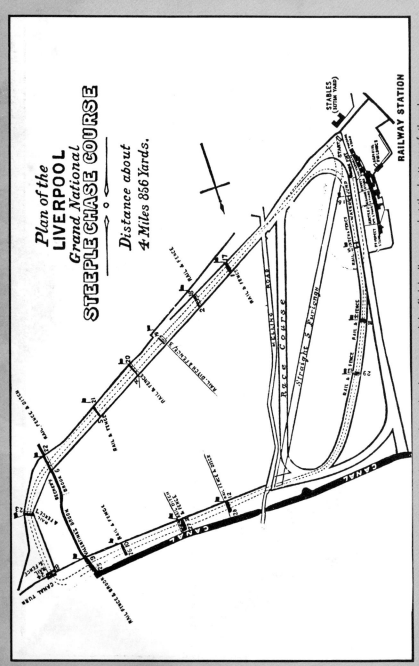

The course, showing the grandstands, the start and the finish all grouped at the bottom of the plan

Becher's Brook, nearly five feet high, over three feet wide and the 'brook' on the landing side another five-and-a-half feet. The drop is thirteen inches, and these 'drop fences' are a key reason why the National is so difficult

A 1930s' back view of the Jockey Club at Newmarket. Left is the members' Victorian sleeping quarters and the main building is in the background

The committee room at the Jockey Club, an old photograph which evokes the atmosphere still

The Lord Manton, DL, Senior
Steward of the Jockey Club over the
period of the Appeal

Captain J. Macdonald-Buchanan,
MC, DL, who in 1982 launched the
Appeal as the then Senior Steward

Christopher Collins, Esq, chosen by
the Club to head Aintree
Racecourse Limited

The Lord Willoughby de Broke,
MC, AFC, AE, K St J, twice a
Steward of the Club, first rode a
winner in 1929

Mrs Mirabel Topham, who ran the Grand National for years, in the paddock at Aintree

Lord Wigg, who said the Jockey Club could end up like a dinosaur — stuffed

Bill Davies, Esq, who bought Aintree and the National from Mrs Topham and tried to sell it to the Jockey Club

The Lord Vestey, chosen by the Jockey Club to save the Grand National

The Earl of Derby, MC, chairman of
the Trustees of the Appeal

J. R. Henderson, Esq, MBE, who first
negotiated with Bill Davies on behalf
of the Jockey Club

The Lord Howard de Walden, TD,
who when Senior Steward said power
was the name of the game

Major-General J. A. d'Avigdor-
Goldsmid who was incensed when
the BBC appeared to criticize the
nobilities of the Turf

The logo for the Appeal was given free to the Campaign by the designer David
Bernstein of Creative Business. However, his suggestion for a slogan was
turned down as undignified: 'Save Aintree before it Ain't'

Although Velvet is of ordinary origins, she is by no means an ordinary person. She thinks poetical thoughts and wants to be 'putting the horse into history'. Mi Taylor says 'She's got little hands like piano wires. I've never seen such a creature on a horse.' One could say the same for many of the great National riders – Fred Winter, Dick Francis and Champion in our own day, ordinary, but not ordinary.

Like all Grand National heroes, Velvet has some quality which the crowd worship, and they mob the National Hunt Committee rooms and tell them 'You tick her off and we'll cut your livers out.'

But, having lifted Velvet up among the gods, the public 'could stand no more. Dead news like dead love has no phoenix in its ashes' and before long Velvet's story is dead. Possibly then its fundamental attraction is that it is a story which has the greatest possible appeal for a short while, and then disappears until the following year. It is a flash in the pan. A moment of transitory greatness.

National Velvet, at any rate, seems not to be transitory. The book was reprinted in 1957, 1958, 1959, 1961, 1962, 1965, 1967, 1970, 1974 and 1980. It still sells a couple of thousand copies a year. Perhaps more people remember the film than the book: with Elizabeth Taylor, the child star of 1944, and Mickey Rooney, which is so frequently re-issued.

Another feature which *National Velvet* has in common with the real Grand National is this – that extraordinary, almost unbelievable things happen and yet are, to the spectators, believable. Year after year the strangest things happen – for example, Devon Loch's fall, or only one horse finishing, or the winner not having a jockey. This is not true of other races, which are much more predictable, as the odds show, and it is not true of other sports, or not to the extent that it is true of the National. Miss Bagnold chose an extraordinary heroine, an extraordinary horse, and extraordinary trainer, and wrote about it all as if it were taking place in a dream.

Perhaps that is the secret of the Grand National; it is everyone's dream, to win the National, and those who win seem to be taking part in that dream.

There is an alternative clue, and a much crueller one, to the fascination of the National, which has to do with the more basic attributes of human nature. A journalist covering the first race in 1839 wrote, 'All men of ardent feelings love moderate danger for the very excitement which it produces, and the intrepidity which it brings into action.'

Is this really the reason for the popularity of the National, a human ghoulish interest in the dangerous, like a public hanging only less predictable and more exciting?

This has its other side, with critics in full cry when disaster strikes. The original Stone Wall fence was heavily criticized, and so was the Canal Turn in 1928 when about twenty horses fell. There have been other nasty accidents since, and a justified outcry coupled with a renewed effort by those who did not believe that the National should continue to be run at all.

There could be some correlation between the number of runners and the possibility of an incident. In the 1837 race there were only 6 runners and the average over the next five years was 13. Gradually the numbers inched up to the twenties and in 1850 it was over 30 for the first time, but fell back to the twenties again virtually through until 1875 and from then until 1891 it was never over 20. Sometimes it was as low as 10. It hovered around the mid-twenties until 1921 when there were 35 runners, in 1928 it was 42 and then a disastrous 66 in 1929. The following year it was still over 40 and in 1947 it was back up to 57, since when the thirties and forties have been the norm.

Yet the years which have had some of the worst accidents – for example four horses killed in 1954 – have not been big fields – twenty-nine in that case. John Hislop who rode four different horses in the National says that while the fences are big, they are 'fair', by which he means they can all be jumped by a hunter at racing pace. He points out that while only a small number of runners complete the course (the odds are 3–1 or 4–1 against doing so) by no means all of them fall. Despite this, he urges that Stewards 'issue an official request to owners and trainers to ensure, as far as possible, that only horses suitable to the National fences, are started for the race, are in a fit condition to run'.

Dick Francis also claims that Aintree is a comparatively safe course. Few jockeys are ever badly hurt, and no more horses die there than anywhere else, although they are given more publicity. 'Liverpool is not a cruel course,' he claims, and he also uses the expression that it is 'fair'. Above all, he says, there is plenty of room. The first five fences are so wide that twenty-five horses could jump them abreast without coming to any harm.

The loose horse is a feature of the National, due to the large number of falls, and J.K. Pye says 'such a horse invariably follows this pattern; having got to the head of the field and acquired a lead of some two or three lengths, he will gallop on in the most resolute fashion . . . the loose horse will look everything a horse should look as it approaches a fence. The ears will be pricked, the nostrils flared, the stride will shorten slightly as he measures the fence, and then at the very last second as though someone had whispered in his ear, "it's a drop fence", he will sheer off to the right or left . . . to collide with the first of the oncoming horses.'

With all these difficulties some owners have been noticeably reticent about entering their horses for the National. Without doubt the image of the race is that it is a dangerous enterprise for horses. Arkle never ran in the Grand National, and plenty of other owners felt like his.

So we have the expert owner and trainer holding back from the race; we have the expert horseman objecting when there is a disaster and the rules have to be changed or the course modified; finally we have those who consider the race itself distasteful and synonymous with animal cruelty. This last group is not really very active, finding hunting, it seems, a much more fruitful field for their protests. The League against Cruel Sports, for instance, contents itself with an occasional letter to the Jockey Club, and concentrates its energies on the fox. There are also those who find the race synonymous with the cruel treatment of horses by their jockeys – this goes back to 1870 when the RSPCA took out a writ against a jockey for excessive whipping and spurring.

Physically, what kind of horse would one buy in the hope that he would win the National? Irish probably and certainly a gelding (mares have rarely won the National). So one would pop over to Dublin, to one of Goff's autumn sales, and run an eye over the available beasts looking for an unbroken three-year-old. The original thoroughbred racehorse, we are told, had a remote ancestor Eohippus, a small quadruped about the size of a fox. Its descendants have become bigger year by year. In 1700, the average size was 13 hands 3 in., according to Admiral Rous, and it has increased an inch every twenty-five years since, so that now the bulk of the winners of the National are about 16 hands, although they have ranged from 15 to 17 hands. But it is a popular fallacy to suppose that only an exceptionally tall horse will get over those fences, so it is no good looking merely for a sizeable animal. Only the most experienced will know exactly what to look for, and the answer is certainly not reflected in the price because winners of the National have changed hands from £2.10s upwards. Here then are a few tips, which, if followed may well lead to success – or may not. Dick Christian, a Melton Mowbray rider of the 1800s gave the following description of the ideal hunter, which may be what we want in the National runner: 'the horse has a great rump, hips and hocks', he said, 'forelegs well afore him and good shoulders, but none of your high short horses' (by which he meant a short body and long legs, which would be no good for jumping at speed). Coming to modern times, Arkle, whose owner, Anne Duchess of Westminster, would never enter him for the National, is described by Peter Willett in his book *The Thoroughbred* like this: 'Every inch of his body expressed strength and hardness. He was broad in the chest and deep of body, which was set on short legs with great bone below the knee. His quarters were slightly sloping, his forearms and second thighs had tremendous muscular development; and the quarters had a prominent ridge of muscle across their highest part, just behind the loins, which is found in many good chasers, and is known as the "jumping bump".'

Arkle was certainly a great horse, but in terms of the record Golden Miller was the greater chaser, as he won the Cheltenham Gold Cup five times and the National once, so a close study of his photograph would not be a waste of time. Agreed Golden Miller did not win at Aintree a second time, but he may well have felt that he had done his bit for Dorothy, and did not want to face the course again. After all, few of the horses that are entered for the National would jump the course in cold blood, willingly. And most of the winners are once-in-a-lifetime affairs. Turning now to the real, live horseflesh, we must, as we've said, discount mere size, but good limbs make a good horse, so here it is vital to look long and hard at the bone structure, the proportions and the angles of the bones. The key word to mutter to the trainer is 'conformation' of which a crude definition might be the way the limbs are set on the body.

Next, look the horse straight in the eye because a nice full eye goes a long way to indicating his temperament and this is a vital factor in a winner. Without a good temperament you've usually got nothing, although it must be said that the temperament of horses has improved greatly over recent years as they are so much better handled from birth. The nasty kicking variety are not nearly as common as they were – and a placid and easily-managed horse may well be a good chaser. You want a competitive horse, but that does not mean he has to have a brutish temperament since horses that are any good are herd creatures, born in a herd, and will therefore have the competitive spirit not only bred but born in them. A bold eye will probably also indicate plenty of self-confidence.

It is, of course, vital not to be sold an unsound horse. Thoroughbred horses are not as sound now as they used to be, due to thirty or more years of intensive commercial breeding which has weakened the strain and the constitution.

The horse that has tired tissues through jumping over long distances, perhaps making bad landings, will of course be spotted by the trainer, nevertheless there are a lot of such horses about, and the expert who expressed the view that half the horses in the National now have something or other wrong with them was probably not exaggerating.

Once the horse is purchased, the next question is what to do with him, for although he can simply be handed over to the trainer of one's choice (who incidentally should most definitely have been in the party at Goff's and had a hand in the selection) he, the trainer, will not necessarily be able to pull off the trick of moulding a National winner.

There are two broad routes to follow, although plenty of cross traffic between them. The one is professional National Hunt steeplechasing and hurdling, according to the Rules, which now include a Jockey Club mandate that the entrant's mares must be in the book, (i.e. must be thoroughbred). The other is hunter steeplechasing and point-to-pointing. A horse which has been hunted regularly will obtain a certificate from one of the 180-odd

Masters of Fox Hounds to entitle him to be entered for the hunter steeplechase (although it is said that some horses from trainers' yards merely 'catch the Master's eye' and slip home again to avoid the hazards of the day's hunting).

Point-to-points, organized by the hunts, now attract some 3,000 horses in the three-month season starting in February, and the racing is sometimes close to professional National Hunt standards. Country-wide attendance, almost half a million people, make the operation commercial by covering the cost of the site and providing the hunt with up to £5,000. The rough-and-tumble of the hunting-field will have been of great value to a horse which is to be raced, and the ex-professionals who have switched from National Hunt to point-to-points also add a competitive element which may be new to the horse which has been hunted.

It is quite possible for the promising horse to go from this programme direct to novice steeplechasing and hurdling.

Much depends on the age of the animal. National Hunt horses may enter hurdling races in the autumn of their third year (remember all horses are 'born' on 1 January), while the Rules allow horses to run in steeplechases from the summer of their fourth year, although few do so before they are five.

Despite the fact that the horse may have been an astonishing bargain, the programme ahead for the new owner can fairly be described as a spending spree. There is the horse's keep, the vet's bills, the cost of the hunt, trainer's fees – and all these bills are coming in monthly. On the other side of the account, if a racing regime has commenced, the chances of winning once in the first year, are less than 2–1. And should the owner be lucky, he must give 10 per cent of the winnings to the trainer, 7½ per cent to the jockey, and reserve 2½ per cent for the stable lad. Some owners minimize the costly upkeep by forming syndicates to buy a horse. Since the Jockey Club turned down Tunbridge Wells as a corporate owner, the limit has been twelve individuals per horse.

The Benson Report in the 1960s estimated that owners of National Hunt horses ought to be able to recover a fair proportion of the costs of keeping a horse in training, but they recognized that this was not now the case, and only a lucky few would recover half what they laid out. One point they specifically noted was that owners should be able to pay their staff adequate wages. 'The remuneration and rewards paid to jockeys, stable lads and other staff should be such as to keep them from the temptations which will sometimes be offered to them.' For what is perhaps an extreme view of these occasional temptations let us pause to see what Barry Brogan, famous National Hunt jockey for ten seasons, wrote on the subject in his book *The Barry Brogan Story*. 'Few jockeys, if any, are working without a punter close at hand filling his pockets . . . A punter likes to know what is "fancied" or "unfancied" in as many races as possible. Armed with this privileged information, he then invests large sums of money on the right horse, or, if a bookmaker, he can lengthen or shorten the odds, depending on the information he has received.

'Rewards from punters to jockeys can vary from paid holidays on the Mediterranean to expensive cars, colour television sets and substantial sums of money which are always handed over discreetly at an inconspicuous rendezvous in untraceable cash.

'Frankly if some jockeys relied solely on the money they earn from mounts and winners, they could never hope to attain the standard of living they enjoy. They make it possible only by breaking the Rules and supplying an endless stream of confidential information to people who are willing to pay high fees for the goods.

'Commercial punting is now so prevalent in Britain that if every jockey who participates were brought before the Jockey Club . . . I'm in no doubt that the whole racing circus would come to an abrupt and embarrassing halt. When Peter Smiles said punting of this sort was worse than dope, he wasn't exaggerating. What astounds one is how jockeys can continue to get away with it day after day. Local stewards must be blind.'

To return to the economics of National Hunt racing, one of the factors here is that, unlike the flat fraternity, the owner is unlikely to make money out of breeding, for the very good reason that his horse will have most likely been gelded. This does not result in any effeminacy of performance; on the contrary the gelding is normally far braver than the stallion. As regards speed, National horses go nearly as fast as those in the Derby, and they keep on doing it for 4½ miles, instead of one-third that distance, and jump thirty fences while they are at it. The reason for gelding a horse is that horses are highly sex-conscious after the age of four, and a horse therefore would be much more likely to have its mind on the fillies than on the fences. The Irish geld horses while still yearlings, using an anaesthetic, and this is apparently painless and uncomplicated. Gelding a horse after it is three years old is, however, a more complex matter, which the animal is unlikely to take in his stride, so to speak.

One advantage which the National Hunt owner has over his flat-racing confrere is the long season. Due to the mild climate which we enjoy, and the considerable amount of rain which keeps the turf soft, he can race almost throughout the year, with only July closed to him, although many of the best chasers are rested until October.

Once the horse of one's choice has begun to race, and it is hoped, to win, the aim must be to enable it to qualify so that it enters the National. Of course, there is the remote possibility that a horse can be purchased which has already qualified in the hands of a previous owner, but more likely this has to be one of the chores of the budding National winner. The qualifications, as the Clerk of the Course at Liverpool described them, are so abstruse that you would have to be a classical scholar to understand them. Nevertheless, on average fifty or more horses are able to achieve the qualifications to enter each year.

8: Dramatis Personae

Horseracing is derived from warfare, chariot racing and the chase, and perhaps it is significant that Queen Boadicea and her warlike people lived on Newmarket Heath. The people in this story follow a tradition of conflict which may have been the more virulent because it was inherently a class conflict:

Lord Sefton versus Mirabel Topham
Lord Leverhulme versus Bill Davies
The Jockey Club versus Lord Wigg
Lord Vestey versus Bill Davies

It is doubtful whether this clash of the classes was purely fortuitous, nor is it certain whether the combatants had some subtle long-term plan for the National or not. One well-known critic of the Jockey Club thought that whatever they did, it was not subtle. An ex-schoolmaster, he said, 'You might say such fuddled thinking is incredible, but it doesn't surprise me. When it comes to brainpower, the Jockey Club is still in the first form.' Be that as it may, Prince Bismarck had remarked to Disraeli that 'You will never have a revolution in England as long as you keep up your racing.' It could therefore be that racing provides the battlefield on which the classes can conduct their warfare, thus sublimating any more virulent forms of revolution to which they might otherwise be attracted.

(These brief biographical notes follow the style of Alan Watkins in being written in the past tense, whether the subjects are alive or not.)

Bill Davies

It was difficult to imagine big, burly, bearded Davies as a child, but he had been one, born in 1936 at Fazakerley, a mile or so around the corner from Aintree. He was born in humble circumstances, and could be said to have had a small chip on the shoulder in consequence.

He left school at fifteen, became a joiner, and a plasterer, the two basic trades in the building business, and set about building garages. By 1960 he had saved £10,000 from the proceeds of a bungalow-building spree, based on a small overdraft with which he bought the land, and in that year he formed Walton Building Company and set himself the target of becoming a millionaire. Ten years later he had become so successful that he effectively pulled out of housing and went into property investment.

He seems always to have been a difficult man, getting involved in lawsuits, getting caught taking more than the permitted £50 out of the country, getting into the hands of the receivers, but despite all this he was claiming by the mid-seventies that he had an overdraft of £6m and assets of £18m. He could rightly be called flamboyant.

This was the time of his deal with Mrs Topham. Why did he do it? Certainly he had ideas for developing the land, but perhaps too he had ideas of becoming respectable and being acceptable. Even in Liverpool, property deals in the sixties and seventies necessitated some colourful behaviour and Bill Davies was beginning to wish to be a different fish. For example, it was at this time that he moved to Mayfair, believing, like Lord Manton, that that was where the action was. It wasn't, not for him, and he retreated to the Wirral. At the same time he bought a racehorse with the unfashionable name of Wolverhampton. But what's in a name? Wolverhampton did not prosper, despite a promising start, winning his first at Wolverhampton races. Bill, flushed with success, said (using the royal 'we'), 'We are in horseracing now and we might as well do things properly. We are told it is a good horse.' Alas he had little chance to prove his claim, and after falling in the National at the twenty-fourth fence, it died. Its trainer was Red Rum's, so it had had every prospect.

Bill was chagrined when the racing fraternity failed to warm to him, and the Jockey Club squabbled, so he decided to give up Aintree. More chagrin still, when Ladbrokes would only offer him £1m for what he had paid £3m for, and when all his later Aintree deals fell through. So in a sense, when Lord Wigg suggested the Jockey Club should take over, it was a godsend. He had hardly imagined himself sitting in Slaughter and May, surrounded by nearly twenty lawyers, lunching in Cazanove's with Henderson; it was heady stuff, despite only being worth £4m. But what kept Bill awake at nights was the question, 'Will they ever give me the money?'

The Earl of Derby

Lord Derby, family motto 'Without changing', was not only born into an ancient earldom, but was also, on his mother's side, a Cadogan and a Chelsea. Like most members of the Jockey Club he was at Eton and Oxford, and, when the war came, in the Grenadier Guards. He became a major and won the Military Cross in the field for his part in the fighting at the Anzio beachhead.

After the war, he returned to the family estates and in 1948 married Lady Isabel Milles Lade, who had been a notable beauty. The wedding, in Westminster Abbey, was attended by the King, the Queen, Princess Elizabeth, Princess Margaret, the Princess Royal, and the Duchess of Kent.

The family name is Stanley, and he not only had a house of that name at Newmarket but also the Stanley and Woodland Studs there.

He inherited the stud from his father, who had revived it in the 1890s and had bred and raced the winners of all the great races in the Calendar. There, they had bred three winners of the Derby. The stud was a considerable financial burden, with Lord Derby describing it as 'a total disaster in recent years' and he had considerable difficulty in keeping the family properties going.

He inherited a vast estate, Knowsley, near Liverpool, and many estates round about. In his youth it was the scene of many lavish parties. An author wrote that more good ale was drunk there than in any hall in England. He sold 900 acres near Ormskirk and 4,775 acres near Macclesfield and then in the middle 1950s sold an 8,800-acre estate near Blackpool to the Church Commissioners. In 1963 he moved out of the 200-room Knowsley Hall into a small house overlooking a lake in the grounds. All this, and the opening of the house to the public, was a result of economic pressure, which eventually caused him to call on the aid of the Chipperfields to set up a wildlife and game reserve to attract bigger crowds. Chipperfield had performed a similar service by establishing so-called safari parks for Lord Bath, the Duke of Bedford, Lord Greton and Sir John Muir. Lord Derby also sold a Rembrandt to the National Gallery, and later a Poussin to the Walker Art Gallery in Liverpool for £1m.

Whether these financial problems should all be ascribed to horse-breeding expenses is hard to say; the Earl also had a reputation for gambling at cards.

Thirteen of the previous eighteen earls had been Lord-Lieutenants of Lancashire, but John Derby resigned the office, infuriated by the government's treatment of the territorials and the way they had brushed aside the nominations he made for knighthoods for leading figures.

Among his idiosyncrasies was a dislike of pianos. He refused to have any at Knowsley. If he was staying away from home and saw a piano, it is said he would lock it up and throw the key into the garden.

By the early 1950s he had had three heart attacks and these left him a pallid figure, smiling in a melancholy way as the world passed by. He dressed in a dapper manner, and might easily have been mistaken for a well-to-do American visitor, who had stepped out of the pages of P.G. Wodehouse. Like many Wodehouse characters, his passion was golf.

John Henderson

'Johnny' Henderson, born 1920, attended Eton and Cambridge and became a stockbroker. He eventually became a partner in that grandest of brokers, Cazenoves, where his son also worked, and a director of Barclays Bank. During the war he was a major in the 12th Royal Lancers, and ADC to Field Marshal Lord Montgomery from 1942 to 1946, from whom he acquired a somewhat terse, but not unkindly, manner. Although he said that only once in the war did he feel justified in waking Monty in the night, he was certainly not afraid of him as the following anecdote demonstrates. He wrote a paper for Montgomery who said, 'I can't imagine how it is that anyone such as yourself who has been with me so long, could write such unmitigated rubbish.' Henderson replied 'You may have your ideas, General, but these happen to be mine.'

His racing colours were Eton-blue hoops, after the old school, and it was somewhat surprising that this was acceptable socially, since OE ties were no longer *de rigeur* after about 1960. Indeed someone seen wearing one in the stockbroker's corridors some years ago was reprimanded. 'We don't wear those in the office, do we?' Henderson rode in point-to-points and hunter chases from the time he left the Army until 1960. His son Nicky was the well-known trainer at Lambourn.

In the early 1980s he became one of Lord Abergavenny's aides at Ascot and it was somewhat surprising that when Abergavenny retired, Henderson was passed over. He was a tough but fair man whose principles showed more prominently than many of his fellow club-members.

Capt. J. Macdonald-Buchanan

Captain 'Johnny' Macdonald-Buchanan did two stints as Senior Steward of the Jockey Club, first from 1969 to 1972 (when he was in his mid-forties) and again from 1979 to 1982. He was educated at Eton, and although unable to join his regiment until towards the end of the war, was in time to win the Military Cross.

The family money came from James Buchanan's whisky distillery, and this enabled him to live in comfort in a largish house in the Cotswolds near Stow-on-the-Wold, and also like many members of the Club to have a London pad in Belgravia. He was a very young member of the Jockey Club, being elected when he was only thirty-one. His brother was also a member of the Club.

In appearance he was a typical soldier, good-looking, with well-brushed hair and moustache, but his crisp manner concealed a strong sense of humour and the ability to get things done diplomatically. He served on the Levy Board, as a Jockey club representative, for several years at the end of the Wigg era.

Lord Manton

Lord Manton was educated at Eton where he was known as 'Soapy'. He served in the Life Guards from 1942 to 1947, and in 1951 rejoined the Army for five years in the 7th (Queen's Own) Hussars. From 1947 to 1964 he rode as an amateur mostly under National Hunt rules and point-to-points, winning about 130 races, mostly in the latter.

He was elected to the Jockey Club in 1968 and served as one of its representatives on the Horserace Betting Levy Board, 1970–75.

He farmed the land round Haughton Hall, in Yorkshire, the ancestral home, but was not a tycoon and could not be called a rich man, although he managed to keep a few racehorses. *Private Eye*, the satirical magazine, was not impressed by his intellect and told the story, which may be apocryphal, that he expressed the desire to formulate a second opinion on a Jockey Club issue. Someone asked, 'How can a man who has never had a first opinion express a second opinion?' In appearance, he was tall and tweedy and looked thoroughly horsey and thoroughly thoroughbred. He always looked privately amused and had the upper-class facility of speaking without moving his jaw.

Sir Desmond Plummer

Sir Desmond Plummer was a chartered surveyor who rose to become leader of the Greater London Council after local government service starting in the mid-1950s. He unexpectedly rocketed into the racing world due to the illness of Sir Stanley Raymond whom he succeeded as Chairman of the Horserace Betting Levy Board in 1974. He had a modest, technical education, but had done well in the Royal Engineers, and as his political career flourished he acquired the trappings of affluence – membership of Lloyds, membership of the Carlton Club and membership of the MCC, conveniently close to his St John's Wood home. He was made a life peer in 1981.

His friends in the Conservative Party arranged his Levy Board appointment although he had no previous connections with racing and while his politics might have been expected to endear him to the Jockey Club, it did not, because 'he was not one of us'.

He worked only a three-day week at the Levy Board and made no revolutionary change.

When Plummer retired, to be succeeded by another mandarin, Sir Ian Trethowan, *The Times*, not given to gossip, said that Lord Plummer was thought to aspire to membership of the Jockey Club. 'He has almost made it. As chairman-designate of the Portman Building Society, he will shortly be occupying premises next door to those of the Club in Portman Square.'

Earl of Sefton

The seventh Earl of Sefton was educated at Harrow and Sandhurst and served in the Horse Guards from 1918 to 1930, travelling to Canada and to India as ADC to the Viceroy. He was Lord-in-Waiting to King Edward VIII and his family held similar Royal posts. He was a keen racing man and a Senior Steward of the Jockey Club. He wrote in *Who's Who* that he owned 34,000 acres.

It is not clear why he sold Aintree in 1949 to Mirabel Topham. Can it have been because he owned two racecourses, the other being Altcar, where the Waterloo Cup was run? More likely he was strapped for cash, because in 1947 he had already sold the Kirkby estate, which had been in his family since the Norman Conquest, Liverpool Corporation being the buyer at £375,000. A short time later, he sold 1,000 acres of his Croxteth estate, also to Liverpool, who kindly left him with the use of most of it. On his death in 1972 his wife, an American divorcee whom he married quietly in 1941, was to leave the rest of the estate's 500 acres, and the Hall, to Liverpool.

A newspaper wrote at his death that he was a star of that pre-war tiny world of Guards officers, amateur jockeys, witty actresses and beautiful maharanees who set their own trends. He wore his check suits close-fitting, as if they were a uniform, and his Horse Guards uniforms as if they were ordinary suits. The story went that when he was quartered at Knightsbridge cavalry barracks after Dunkirk, a staff officer inspecting the barracks to see if they knew their role in the event of invasion asked, 'Enemy-parachuted troops are holding the Serpentine bridge and Park Lane. What would you do?' 'I'd send for the military,' replied Sefton without a smile.

Lord Vestey

Every schoolboy knows that Lord (Sam) Vestey was the spokesman for a rich family whose members were said to have paid virtually no tax for sixty years. Like the majority of members of the Jockey Club, Sam Vestey was educated at Eton, where he was unfortunately known as 'Spam' Vestey probably because his was not an ancient aristocratic line. The family fortunes were founded by two brothers, William and Edward, who, like Sam, were in the middle of a tax controversy back in the 1920s. Trying to explain his tax system to the Commissioners, one of the brothers claimed, 'I am technically abroad' and it is believed he meant that he lived technically in Brazil. This did not stop him paying Lloyd George a sum, alleged to be £25,000, for his peerage. King George V, disgusted, wrote to his Prime Minister, 'I cannot conceal from you my profound concern at the very disagreeable situation which has arisen on the question of honours.' Lloyd George replied, 'With regard to Sir William Vestey, I regret that in this case, the evidence he had given before the Commissioners of Income Tax had not been drawn to my attention.'

Be all that as it may, the family prospered, to put it mildly. Sam, whose father had been killed in battle in Italy when he was only three years old, was thirty when in the late sixties he inherited the two £1-shares which gave him with his cousin Edmund control over the mighty empire which even the *Financial Times*, hardly an organ of exposure, called 'very private'. For more than eighty years, the Vestey family had successfully kept themselves out of the public eye, and Sam and Edmund planned to keep up that tradition until *The Sunday Times* Insight team came along and exposed their tax contributions.

Today, the organization is a conglomerate, composed of one of the world's most integrated meat businesses, from live cattle to the Dewhurst 'master butcher' chain, and, on the side, insurance, shipping and guard dogs. Its sales are said to be over £300m annually, and book assets (very conservatively valued, says the *Financial Times*) are about £50m. By means of various family trusts, Vesteys control three shipping lines, three ranching businesses which lease 20,000 sq. miles in Australia and own 2,000 sq. miles in Brazil plus 1,000 sq. miles in Venezuela.

Land, cattle, slaughter-houses, cold stores, ships, shops and Britain's largest meat importing and wholesaling business all under their private control.

So no wonder they were careful about tax. According to *The Times*, Dewhursts paid only £10 tax on profits of £4.1m in 1979, but this was nothing to what the family was supposed to have saved by discovering 'loopholes' for their private wealth. Sam defended the position, 'Nobody pays more tax than he has to. We are all tax dodgers aren't we?' His personal fortune is estimated (by the newspapers) at £50m and he has houses in Gloucestershire (4,500 acres), Belgravia and Scotland (where the family have 100,000 acres).

After a spell in the Guards, Sam Vestey began to live the life of a country gentleman, taking up polo and doing good works such as becoming President of the Gloucestershire Association of Boys' Clubs and County President of the St John's Ambulance Brigade. In 1981 he married for the second time, his bride being Celia Knight, a keen horsewoman who happened to have a horse called Sam.

The Vesteys were rarely out of the public eye once the tax scandal had burst. The general public's attitude was one of uncertainty mingled with distrust. The columnist Bernard Levin, writing in *The Times*, put it quite well when he wrote about what he called the Affaire Vestey. He asked, 'Is it possible to admire what the Vesteys did? I think not . . . You may not condemn the Vesteys, but you cannot with a straight face hold them up as admirable and worthy citizens, and their behaviour as worthy of emulation.'

A Scottish MP also attacked him in the Commons. He said they had acquired an estate of 100,000 acres and the Treasury had agreed to waive the liability for capital transfer tax in return for limitations on development and agreements on public access. He said the Vestey family was notorious for attaching feudal conditions limiting the use of land. Somewhat more contentiously he claimed that they acquired the land for the sole purpose of surrounding themselves with large areas of emptiness in which they and their friends could disport themselves two or three times a year chasing the stags over the crags. 'Sometimes one wished,' he said, 'they had followed the stags over the crags and the land could be returned to public ownership.' It was naughty of him to get the matter out of proportion; two Cowdrays are said to own 250,000 acres in Scotland.

Somehow this uncertainty about the Vesteys attached itself to Sam himself. One minute he would be all smiling and charming and another he would be in a mood of suppressed black anger, his eyes rolling and flashing as his mighty frame appeared about to burst out of his suit. A psychologist might well have been able to make something of it – suppressed feelings of guilt perhaps. He was a fearless sportsman, as his exploits at polo and eventing illustrated.

Simon Weatherby

Simon Weatherby was Secretary to the Jockey Club, a position held by a member of his family since 1771, when it had been acquired by rather devious means. He was the last member of his family to hold the post. He was an able administrator who became known among the dinosaurs of the Jockey Club for the cat-like charm with which he attempted to propel them into the twentieth century, or, as he himself said, at least into the nineteenth.

Born in 1938, he was educated at Winchester, a family tradition. Later, he managed to get to America where he attended Columbia University, reading English Literature. His one ambition was to be a writer, and he may well have regretted not having followed this through, but his cousin David died suddenly in his forties in 1972 and Simon inherited the Jockey Club job after spending some years in the family business. He was a great success, much admired by the Turf, although he was by no means a typical member of it.

Sadly, in 1976 he developed a kidney problem and despite several attempts at transplants, he only managed to keep going on the kidney machine. The function of the machine is to get rid of poisons from the blood and Weatherby would have to rush off home perhaps three days a week to put himself on it. A telephone by the machine could be used to call engineers, day or night, in an emergency. The strain told on him and his complexion became more yellow and strained week by week. Nevertheless his courtesy and humour remained undiminished and he worked hard both at the Jockey Club and at home – either his flat in

London or at the typical small country house in a little village on the edge of the Cotswolds near Shipston-on-Stour.

Those who had seen the strain he was under were greatly saddened, but not really surprised when he died of a heart attack shortly after New Year's Day 1983. He left various other Weatherbys in the Jockey Club but none of them able to take over the Secretariat which passed out of the family.

The Lord Wigg

It is sometimes asked what George Wigg knew about racing that qualified him to become one of its leading figures in the 1960s and 1970s and still to speak with authority in the 1980s when he was over eighty.

His addiction to the Turf began as a country boy at Basingstoke and when he joined the Tank Corps as a regular soldier at the age of eighteen (just as World War I ended) and went to the Middle East, one of his first ambitions was to buy a racehorse. He tried to register his racing colours as khaki but was turned down. Let it not be thought that he was rich – after a council-school education, he enlisted in the ranks, although his father had been an officer and his mother born in a barracks. His wife had two brothers who were both professional jockeys.

During his early days in the Army he joined the Labour Party and was a member of the Fabians. He finally left the Army in 1937, to rejoin in 1940 as a lieutenant in the Royal Army Educational Corps, and eventually became a colonel, the only member of the House of Commons to rise from the ranks to rank. So when he burst upon the political scene at the age of forty-five in the first post-war Labour administration, as member for Dudley, he was something of a striking figure.

'What a face!' wrote the *Guardian*. 'Big ears, long nose, and small sharp eyes. A man who always has the air of being "on to a good thing" whether on the racecourse or in politics.' He was the devoted assistant of another character, Emanuel Shinwell, throughout the lifetime of two Attlee governments, and managed Harold Wilson's campaign for the leadership of the Labour Party.

In 1961 he became a member of the Tote Board, a position he resigned on becoming Paymaster-General in 1964. For the next three years he had an office in No. 10 Downing Street where he was said to exercise a profound but mysterious influence. The highlights of his political career had been a passionate interest in newspapers and journalists, in security (he uncovered the Profumo affair) and a passion too for litigation on libel matters. In 1967 he became a peer, and one of his sponsors in the House was Lord Goodman.

He became an owner by paying £500 for a horse called Gout, which raced and raced but never won, and eventually died of a brain tumour. But it was as Chairman of the Horserace Betting Levy Board from 1967 to 1972 that his influence on racing was most marked. It began unpleasantly when the Jockey Club indicated to him that it was his job to collect the levy from the bookmakers, and they would decide how to spend it. He did not agree, and stormed out of their premises. Nevertheless he did a magnificent job in increasing the levy from £2.6m to £4.3m by changing it from a charge on betting to one on bookies' turnover.

There were other less significant brushes with the Club, but all were indicative of a passion for tilting at the Establishment. He found that a fifteen-acre paddock at Newmarket 'perhaps one of the finest paddocks in England' had been taken over for the breeding of pheasants – there were breeding coops all over the place, said Wigg. This paddock was supposed to be the National Stud which the Levy Board acquired in 1963, run for the breeding of horses, not pheasants. He also found that there was a full-time gamekeeper on the staff whose wages were paid jointly by the Jockey Club and the National Stud. As a result, a pheasant shoot conducted by the Jockey Club members at Newmarket 'had to be discontinued'. The Club tried to explain away the employee as a 'vermin exterminator' but he was listed in the phone directory as a keeper. The Club was not amused.

More significantly Wigg saved 600 acres of Epsom Downs for the nation, thus ensuring the future of Epsom. But there was another unpleasant incident in 1969 after which *The Times* said 'Relations between Lord Wigg and the Jockey Club are said never to have been at such a low ebb.' At the Bollinger lunch he compared the Club to a well-kept vintage motor car, interesting for use on the occasional drive if you have infinite time and patience, and willingness to judge the article by its original quality and virtue. Wigg said he did not have infinite patience.

In retaliation, the Duke of Norfolk made the unprecedented step of taking over the public address system at Ascot on a subsequent Saturday, speaking from the unsaddling enclosure, and speaking his mind. He criticized Wigg openly for an astonishing public squabble. Wigg replied that this was a marvellous example of the Duke's bad manners, and said that he was not a vintage motor car, but a horse and buggy.

By 1972, when he retired from the Levy Board, to be succeeded by Sir Stanley Raymond, he was a disillusioned man. 'Racing used to be a pleasant escape. Now there is so little friendliness shown towards me that when I finish [at the Levy Board] I want nothing more to do with the sport. Certain people are so damned rude.'

In 1974 he became President of BOLA, the Betting Offices' Licencees' Association, representing the big four bookies, and in 1975 Ladbrokes named a race after him. In 1976 there was an unfortunate incident when he was charged with using insulting behaviour in the West End, and the magistrate said he rejected Lord Wigg's evidence, but decided his behaviour did not constitute an offence.

Later, he was to play a significant part in the 'saving' of the Grand National, holding out an olive branch to the Jockey Club, which they duly accepted with gloved hand. Such generosity earned the accolade that 'he was an original'. He certainly was a character.

Summing up his career at the Levy Board, Phil Bull, a severe critic of the racing Establishment has written, 'Lord Wigg took charge in a dynamic way, and pushed things in the right direction, insisting upon fixture-list criteria which would maximize the levy. General Sir Randle Fielden, the Senior Steward, had the unenviable job of dragging the Jockey Club along. Between them, Lord Wigg and Gerry Fielden were responsible for the most fruitful years of change in racing's history, and the real credit for it all was Lord Wigg's. George Wigg's arrival at the Levy Board was the best thing to happen to racing in my lifetime. He saved British racing. He's never had that credit acknowledged in any way. Lord Wigg has had the icy-cold shoulder from racing's hierarchy. It's a disgrace. It may be understandable – the Jockey Club being what it is – but it is a disgrace to everyone concerned.'

9: Mirabel

Nothing could be more theatrical than the Grand National. So for it to fall into the hands of a former Gaiety Girl who would dominate it for many years was highly appropriate. About 1843, Lord Sefton, who owned Aintree, had leased the course and the race to a horsebreeder, Edward Topham of Middleham, Yorkshire, who had attracted Sefton's attention by his skill as a handicapper and clerk of the course. The family continued to manage Aintree after Edward died, and the business descended eventually to his grandson Arthur R. Topham. Arthur took no part in the family business, but his wife Mirabel most certainly did.

She was the daughter of an artist who later got a job managing the Haymarket Theatre. This aroused his daughter's interest in the stage, and both Mirabel and her sister took to the boards. Her sister was a Gaiety Girl and Mirabel also became a member of the chorus. Talking about it later she said 'We were not really dancers you know, more of *show pieces*.' She was also said to have been a pantomime star and once claimed to have been a model, adding 'they had more meat on the bone then'. On the legitimate stage she adopted the name Hope Hillier and played with Charles Hawtrey and Seymour Hicks.

Arthur Topham was something of a stage-door Johnny, and it was while Mirabel was playing in *Quality Street* at her father's theatre, the Haymarket, that he met and courted her. In 1922 he persuaded her to leave the stage and marry him. They lived at first in Warwickshire where she always used to claim she 'worked on several committees'. It was not clear what this meant, but at any rate her organizing ability became obvious to the older members of the Topham family, who persuaded her and her husband to move in 1935 to Liverpool. Three years later she became chairman and managing director of Topham Ltd and began to put Aintree on its feet. She was a trenchant commentator – 'I never believe in disguising mutton as lamb' she said – and her energetic approach was characterized by the telegraphic address she gave to Aintree – CHASING, LIVERPOOL. Later, she rebuilt a derelict cottage on the racecourse as her home, Paddock Lodge, which for some reason she called 'Padlocked Lodge', and she also claimed to have built a grandstand out of a rubble-tip.

Physically she was formidable, described as a woman of imposing stature, with a fondness for good tweeds and astonishing hats. She claimed not to enjoy lavish entertaining. 'I prefer a simple picnic.' But she must have enjoyed her food and was known as the fourteen-stone Queen of Aintree. She had a London house in a Nash terrace in Regent's Park as well as a holiday house in the Isle of Wight.

During the war she adopted the orphaned children of Arthur's cousin, the Bidwells, and James Bidwell was later to change his name by deed poll to Bidwell-Topham in order to take over the business. He became Clerk of the Course in 1956. Mirabel's husband died in 1958 aged seventy-three.

She was always undisputedly in charge of Aintree. She said: 'There was no secret about how I managed to put the place on its feet. If you apply common sense and justice to anything you are bound to get on. It is not so terribly hard. Mind you, things have happened to me in the racing world which we had better leave out. I work as hard as anyone at Aintree. Sometimes I'm still at it in the middle of the night.'

After the 1939–45 war, she set about the uphill task of attracting owners and a reluctant public to Aintree, and she visited Downing Street in person to make sure that the 1946 race would be run. She felt it vital to broaden its appeal, and not to rely on the National alone. One venture, in 1954, was a motor-racing circuit where the European Grand Prix was staged. These meetings continued for seven years during which damage was done to the drainage on parts of the racecourse. But by now Liverpool was football crazy and thousands preferred soccer to the dingy dilapidated stands and barren wastes of Aintree, which was gradually reduced to three-day event centred round the National.

Mirabel claimed she had always wanted to go into theatrical production. 'It teaches you to take the rough with the smooth. It is lucky for the public that my husband did not have a theatre because Heaven knows what I might have inflicted on them.'

The Sunday Times summed her up like this. 'A woman of exceptionally forceful personality, who would probably find it intolerable to work with a strong-minded subordinate of independent views. Vigorous, outspoken, and with a very real sense of the value of money, she is in many respects ideally qualified to be a successful business woman, particularly as she has a hidden reserve of charm. Unfortunately, a streak of obstinacy, perhaps a virtue in itself, has meant that even in cases where she has been clearly in the right, she sometimes managed to give the impression that she was largely in the wrong.'

One example of this was when she quarrelled with the BBC and ended up by supplying her own commentators for the Grand National broadcast, which afforded many listeners a great deal of hilarity. Her gateman had to improvise for ten minutes when the start was delayed and the winner was announced as having fallen at the first fence.

Another, and much more significant act, was her sudden individual decision in 1964 to sell Aintree for £900,000 to Capital and Counties Property Co. for building houses for 15,000 people on the racecourse, which would, she said, never again stage the Grand National. The outcry was enormous. Lord Derby said 'This is the most staggering piece of news I have ever heard [surely an exaggeration?]. I understand that Mrs Topham said everyone knows that racing is in a sorry state. This is the most utter nonsense I have ever heard [another exaggeration?].' Mrs Topham blamed racing costs and falling attendances at Liverpool and hoped to move the race (now registered under a protective company) to another site.

Lord Sefton, a wartime Senior Steward of the Jockey Club, whose ancestor had leased the course to the Tophams, and who had himself sold the course to Mirabel in 1949 for £275,000 on the advice of his accountant, immediately leapt into the fray. He was sensitive to his position in Liverpool as there had been a hoax played in 1944 when he was elected Lord Mayor of the City when a Conservative nominator made him out as a hero who had marched from El Alemein to Tunis. As Captain the Earl of Sefton had never left the United Kingdom during his wartime Army service, this caused embarrassment.

He brought an action against Tophams and Capital on the grounds that the conveyance of 1949 stated that during the lifetime of Lord Sefton, Tophams were not to cause or permit Aintree to be used other than for horseracing under Jockey Club rules and not to build. He claimed that in December 1963, Mrs Topham had come to see him with tears in her eyes begging to be released from this covenant because Aintree was not paying. He told her that he was not going to discuss it – he did not discuss business matters with her. The end of racing at Aintree seems inconceivable, he said. It would alter his whole way of life. It would be an appalling idea to millions. Tophams had mismanaged Aintree and we were on the threshold of a boom for racing. And so on.

Lord Justice Stamp granted injunctions to restrain Tophams and Capital from going ahead with their plans. The two companies appealed but in May 1965 their appeal was dismissed by the Court of Appeal, although they were given leave to go to the House of Lords. For the first of many times, Mirabel announced that the next Grand National would be the last, and prepared once again to put in a personal appearance at court, this time alone, as the property company had decided to give up any further legal action. By a decision of three to two, the Law Lords allowed Topham's appeal. Much hinged on the words 'not to cause or permit' the land to be used for other purposes than horseracing. Lord Sefton was ordered to pay £30,000 costs. Mirabel said 'Tophams always understood they were entitled to act as they did'.

Mr Howell, Minister of Sport, at once said (it was nonsense of course), that 'it will be possible to keep the National and open the site 365 days a year for full recreational and sporting uses'. And the chairman of County, Leslie Marley, wrote to *The Times* to explain that '(1) my company does not seek to buy and destroy racecourses nor to scrap races; (2) starting as a sixteen-year-old horse-gunner in World War I, I have had to do with horses all my life – hunting, showing, racing and breeding – and have loved every minute of it.' He added that what was wanted was 'wholehearted support from the Jockey Club in initiating a syndicate to run the racecourse'. He would have to wait twenty years.

In the light of events, it is interesting that Lancashire County Council (precursor of Merseyside) announced at this time that the preservation of Aintree was essentially the responsibility of racing interests. They rejected an application for housing and would turn down any others. While no ratepayers' money would be spent on subsidizing racing there, they would negotiate with Mrs Topham to buy the site for a sports centre or some such purpose. Mirabel reluctantly announced that the race would be staged again in 1967, but she held out for £2m from the Council and their deal for a recreational centre fell through.

By 1968 there was talk of a government-assisted purchase of Aintree, and a non-profit-making trust, of which Mirabel would be a member, to run the race. This too fell through, and there were various other offers for Aintree including one from the Sporting Land Development Company for £2.1m with the public having the right to subscribe for one million £1 shares. This company was one-half a subsidiary of the South African banking concern Schlesingers and one-half owned by an investment company run by two young tycoons. The future of the National would be safeguarded until 1998. Again Mirabel turned them down. Now aged eighty-two, she had said 'I've got all my teeth and I can bite like hell.' Once again she said this would be the last Grand National, and once again the phrase became a joke, but one that did not go down too well in racing circles. It was like the actress making her 'positively final appearance on the stage'.

In 1972, Mrs Topham had met a thirty-eight-year-old Liverpool self-made-man-cum-property-developer, Bill Davies, who had first watched the Grand National as a small boy from outside the course looking through the railings. Nearly two years later she concluded a deal with Davies whereby his company, Walton Group, would buy the course and the race for £3m, with the aim of developing the land. They contracted to run the National for at least five years. At a press conference at the Savoy Hotel to announce the deal, Bill Davies said he did not know if he would get planning permission for a forty-acre shopping site, but he seemed confident, and claimed he wanted to run the race 'for the rest of my life'. Major Peter Beckwith-Smith, clerk of the course until 1956, was coming back to mastermind the next two races, and Davies wanted to reintroduce Grand Prix motor-racing and other year-round attractions. One thing he did not tell the press was that he was borrowing part of the purchase price from the Tophams and it would be a very long time before they got their money – they had not been repaid by the 1983 race.

The Davies deal was finally signed in November and thus ended over one hundred years of the Topham family's connection with Aintree. But even then another squabble sprang up when an Irish racehorse owner and property developer claimed that he had a prior agreement with her and threatened to block the sale. Luckily for Mirabel he did not do so.

There is a story that after the sale, she removed everything from the Stewards' Room. There was no hot water or coal. Mirabel, when taxed on the matter, replied 'Oh, that belonged to Tophams. The coal comes out of my house.' Bill Davies had to bring in the local haberdasher to put things right for the Stewards.

10: Davies as Owner

Bill Davies's love affair with the racing fraternity did not last long. He claimed to know nothing about 'the tairf' as he called it, or said that what he did know would not fill a visiting card. 'I'm an outsider,' he told a columnist. 'I'm a businessman who likes a challenge and my main interest in Aintree is the prestige it brings to my company.' He claimed his company would set up 200 betting shops in the Liverpool area. And why not have a Miss Grand National?

'The trouble with racing is that all the money is creamed off by the bookmakers . . . When I took over Aintree, the bookies were getting a pitch for 75p but we've upped it to £6 and £36 . . . I get on fine with the Jockey Club but I've told them to their face that the £10,000 we get for the National is a disgrace. You go round trying to give people the straight facts and you find yourself in offices full of cocktail cabinets.' But the press condemned him for charging £20 for admission to the members' enclosure. They said he 'was not natural Jockey Club material'.

He retaliated by calling a press conference, announcing that he was being advised by Lazard, and that he would float forty-nine per cent of the racecourse company as a public issue. In 1975, he told journalists he would make a profit of £400,000 on Aintree, against the £20,000 when he took it over from Mrs Topham.

But a very short time indeed passed before Davies was in deep disagreement with the Jockey Club, whom he tried to hold to ransom by laying down his requirements before the next National was held. *The Times* described this as 'pointing the pistol at the head of authority'.

The following day Davies held an impromptu press conference in Liverpool to defend his request for a grant and his plan to stage a £100,000 Aintree Derby. Again *The Times* attacked him: 'What he does not seem to realize is that the Rules of Racing cannot be adjusted simply to suit him, and the allocation of Levy Board funds is agreed only after a great deal of discussion.' They went on: 'He cannot dictate to either the Jockey Club, who are responsible for the Rules of Racing, or the Levy Board.'

Davies said he knew exactly why he did not see eye to eye with the Jockey Club or with its senior Steward, Viscount Leverhulme. 'I went to a secondary school, but I would not have had this trouble if I went to a public school. It's as simple as that. Lord Leverhulme and I are both Liverpudlians, except the difference is, he is more upper-class than I am.'

The Sunday Times said that lack of education or not, Davies at forty years old had done quite well for himself. 'He runs two dark blue Rolls-Royces and has a large detached house in the Wirral, Cheshire, and he estimates conservatively that he has made close on £15m since he left school in a Liverpool suburb, at the age of fifteen, to become a £4-a-week plasterer.' The paper went on: 'there is more than a touch of the philanthropist about the expansive Mr Davies, who has a penchant for large cigars. "Aintree is part of Liverpool," he says. "The Grand National is the greatest race in the world . . . If I get my way, I want the National to go on forever."'

Davies had announced that he could cut the three-day National meeting to a one-day affair, but he eventually backed down 'for the sake of the British people' as he put it. Indeed he seemed to be backing down all round after the 1975 race was run in April, but in fact he was busy behind the scenes negotiating with another buyer. This was an Irish property developer, also fond of cigars, called Patrick McCrea. *The Times* said that Davies's ambition to bulldoze his way to success as the promoter of the National 'had died a foreseeable death'.

Mr McCrea was described, like Mr Davies, as a rags-to-riches operator. After starting life as a ship's cook, he entered the world of property and became a millionaire. Racing was his chief passion in life. Aged thirty-seven (three years younger than Davies) he owned an 150-acre farm in County Neath where he bred cattle and horses. At one time he had forty horses in training carrying his wife's colours, and he had made a bid for Aintree in 1973 when Mrs Topham was selling. He said 'It's the only way to win the Grand National. It is the only way I can do it. I shall be able to hold my own gallops and run my own races.'

But he spoke too soon. The deal fell through and Davies was once more landed with the problem of running the race, and making money on his £3½m investment. The trouble was that he had borrowed £2¾m from the banks to finance the deal. *The Times* claimed that to find the interest on £3m from Aintree was 'absurd'. The total profitability of all the racecourses in the country put together hardly reaches that figure, they said.

'It's very upsetting for the likes of me,' said Davies, referring to the Jockey Club's attitude. So he announced that he would publicly auction Aintree in London. For a brief period the banks foreclosed and a receiver was put in, who offered to sell the course for £2½m. The numerous enquiries ranged from a Japanese restaurateur, who wished to put Red Rum in a Safari Park, to a scrap-metal dealer who went bankrupt.

But meantime he decided to find someone who not only knew something about racing, but would be attracted to the prospect of sponsoring the National. At the suggestion of the editor of *Sporting Life* he talked to Cyril Stein of Ladbrokes, the book-makers, and together they put up a deal for a seven-year contract for Ladbrokes to manage the course at a rent of £250,000 a year. With all the income plus a big TV contract, Stein thought he could not only break even but make money on this basis. And so it proved, although Ladbrokes claimed they never made much out of it. Nevertheless it was good for their standing in racing circles, and at one stage they tried to negotiate a deal to buy Aintree, but Davies's price was always too high for them, despite the rumour that at one point he came close to £4m; there was also talk of a deal with the Levy Board and Ladbrokes putting in £1m, and of a Trust with Ladbrokes offering £2m.

The years of Ladbrokes' regime went slowly by, with Davies taking a back seat, and trying to find a way of obtaining planning permission for development on the course. He had no success and as the 1981 race came to an end the seemingly eternal question was once again raised 'Would 1982 be the last National?' with Ladbrokes retired from the scene.

Davies moaned that his purchase of Aintree had been a 'massive business blunder' and the 'worst deal of his life' and as the last of Ladbrokes' races approached – April 1982 – Davies really put his mind to the future, because high interest rates were now crippling him. One of those with whom he discussed his problem was his old friend George Wigg. He told him that in the twenty years since 1961, the government had taken £150m out of Aintree in tax, of which the Levy Board had had ten per cent.

Should they now put something back?

PART THREE

The Campaign

11: A Public Scrap

In February 1982, just before what was again the 'last' Grand National, two lords of the realm started a public scrap over the future of the race, but it really was the Jockey Club which was at the heart of the row, although, with its usual aplomb, the Club kept mum. Later, an ex-minister joined in the fun, in a more direct attack on the Club.

The Levy Board was led by Lord Plummer, an unpopular man who was, however, anxious to make his mark on British racing. His predecessor at the Levy Board, Lord Wigg, also unpopular in some circles, had the added characteristic of being very unpopular with Lord Plummer, and the two were spoiling for a fight. In the course of 1981, Plummer had met Davies several times, but a key meeting took place on 5 February 1982 at the Board's offices in Holborn. Unknown to Plummer, Davies and Wigg had developed a friendly relationship, dating back to 1975 when the editor of *Sporting Life*, Ossie Fletcher, had brought them together with Cyril Stein, chairman of Ladbrokes, and as a result they had 'saved' the National for a further seven years under Ladbrokes' management.

On the day before Plummer was due to meet Davies, Wigg went to see Willie Whitelaw, the Home Secretary, in his room at the House of Commons, ostensibly wearing his hat as president of BOLA to talk about bookmakers' affairs. But what he really wanted was to forestall Plummer by telling Whitelaw that it was his conviction that Bill Davies would lease Aintree to Race-course Holdings Trust, the Jockey Club subsidiary, for the figure at which Ladbrokes had leased it, £250,000 a year. He urged Whitelaw to put pressure on the Jockey Club to negotiate a deal with Davies. Wigg adopted this rather roundabout approach because he himself hated the Jockey Club which had told him, in 1968 when he was Levy Board Chairman: 'It is up to you to raise the levy, and it is for us to say how it is to be spent.'

On the following day, knowing nothing of all this, Plummer had a two-hour meeting with Davies, hoping to strike a deal to buy Aintree for the Levy Board. Later Davies claimed that Plummer had offered him £3m, and this tallies with a claim by a Board official that if they could raise another £1m they could strike a deal with Davies at the 'realistic' £4m. Plummer also told Davies that he wanted a survey of the Aintree grandstands to see if they were fit for a race meeting, or if they needed a Levy Board investment, and Davies gave permission to carry out an independent survey. Later Davies was to say he believed the Levy Board should run Aintree.

When he heard about this, Wigg went to see Davies who told him 'I've had a gutful of all this. I'm fed up with Lord Plummer. Everyone is making money out of the course – that's worth much more than £8m.' Wigg listened but did not believe all he heard, as he was convinced Davies had paid only £3m plus legal fees. Davies also claimed that he could get planning permission to build a supermarket and houses on the course but Wigg did his best to disillusion him.

Wigg pondered all this on his way back to London and by Sunday he had made up his mind to tackle Plummer head-on by going public with his own proposal. He rang the *Sporting Life* and outlined the proposal he had put to Whitelaw. And he also attacked Plummer who 'had no right' to make such an offer to Davies. 'All this clandestine negotiation by leak and innuendo is a waste of time. Lord Plummer is in no position to deliver anything above the market price – and this is less than £1m. The Treasury simply will not allow any more public money than that to buy it.' A front-page article duly appeared under the banner headline 'Holding Plan to Save the National'. It outlined Wigg's proposal, which seemed practical as Racecourse Holdings Trust already controlled Newmarket, Cheltenham, Market Rasen,

Wincanton and Haydock, and had leases from the local authorities on Nottingham and Warwick racecourses. Wigg went on to blame the Jockey Club member Lord Sefton for all the present troubles, by selling Aintree to Mirabel Topham in 1949. 'As a consequence, Portman Square has a duty to save the course . . . They are amongst the richest men in England and can draw on their reserves.'

Plummer reacted by issuing his own statement to the press. Wigg simply could not make up his mind about Aintree. 'I wish he would – about the Levy Board's role – and then shut up.' He also claimed that Wigg's idea was his anyway.

And finally Davies joined in by claiming that he wanted £1m rental for Aintree, not a quarter of a million. This at last brought a reaction from the Jockey Club. Col. Tommy Wallis, standing on his dignity, said RHT would have to be approached direct and not through the media. 'We have never gone out to find racecourses, they have always come to us.' He described the £1m rent proposal as 'clearly absurd'.

Nothing appeared to happen in the next two weeks. The Jockey Club remained silent. However, a number of other interested parties began to agitate, and on 22 February one of them exploded. He was the Minister of Sport under successive Labour governments through the 1960s and 1970s, Dennis Howell, MP for Birmingham, Small Heath. Howell intensely disliked the Jockey Club and their relationship was now at an all-time low. He was never invited to any of their functions, although as an ex-Minister of Sport this was the least he might have expected. 'They don't like being told the truth about their role and responsibility,' he said.

So he called the press to the Charing Cross Hotel and told them what he thought about the Jockey Club and Aintree. 'Racecourse Holdings Trust have shown no interest up to now. Portman Square is full of apathy and lethargy. They are prepared to see the race go. What they must remember is that every penny in the Levy comes from punters, and not as they seem to think to subsidize livestock.' He put up a proposal to transfer ownership to Merseyside County Council at a price to be determined by the Liverpool City valuer, and then to designate it as a regional sports centre.

'The Jockey Club, Levy Board and Racecourse Holdings Trust

are public trustees for the benefit of racing as a whole. If they don't act in this capacity as regards the Grand National they are quite clearly abdicating their responsibility. They should be held to account for their failure . . . Some members of the Jockey Club wouldn't mind Aintree being closed forever while others are determined to do down Bill Davies at all costs,' he said.

Howell then went out into the car park of Charing Cross station and jumped over a railing for the benefit of the photographers. 'Howell over the hurdles'.

Mr James Stuart-Cole, leader of the Merseyside Council, said he was happy with Mr Howell's proposals and had instructed his council officers to look closely into them. But, now came the rub. 'Funding this to the tune of £1.5m in the present climate would be very difficult.' He really meant impossible.

The Jockey Club's position throughout this period is not easy to define. What Howell said about the 'anti-National' members was true. None of them had wanted Wigg's proposal because they did not like Wigg or his interference. They were predominantly a collection of snobs who disliked Davies and all he stood for. One of them was later to write to Lord Derby describing Davies's company as 'unscrupulous property developers' and this was probably not untypical.

A small number of members of the Club were, however, forming themselves into a group to see if the National could be saved by Racecourse Holdings Trust. As usual the Club maintained absolute secrecy about what it was doing – it had never believed it necessary to justify its actions and this was no time to start. Simon Weatherby, secretary to the Club, told *Sporting Life* 'Neither the Senior Steward nor I can speak for Racecourse Holdings Trust. Although it is a wholly owned subsidiary, it operates entirely independently.' This was nonsense. RHT operates out of the Jockey Club – its Chairman, Johnny Henderson, is a member, its managing director Col. Tommy Wallis, lives, eats and breathes in the Club offices, its finances are administered by the Jockey Club finance department, and it is hard to think of any way in which it operates 'independently'.

The Senior Steward, Capt. Johnny Macdonald-Buchanan, talked with Johnny Henderson and with Lord Derby (John Derby, who had a large estate close to Aintree and considerable interests in the Liverpool district). Henderson was asked to contact Davies and see what could be done. It was agreed that a simple lease to operate the race would not be satisfactory, as this would leave the course in Davies's hands. Henderson also found out that Mirabel Topham had cleverly registered the rights in the race in a separate company, so that any deal to operate the race would be quite separate from any rights over the racecourse. Another factor was the unsatisfactory state of the grandstand and buildings. The Jockey Club (or rather RHT) could not get involved in capital expenditure on repairs work etc., if the racecourse itself was to remain Davies's property.

With these factors in mind, these Jockey Club members settled down to discussing how they could buy Aintree from Davies. How much would it cost, and where would the money come from? The figure made public by Davies was £8m and this was the sum Henderson was quoted. There was no question of finding such a figure from Jockey Club funds; it would have to be raised by private subscription. The Jockey Club did not normally appeal to anyone – least of all the public – but this is what it would have to do.

Alas the government would not now give it high priority. Yet there was a brief flirtation with the Cabinet. The Minister for Sport, Neil Macfarlane, made the curious and unlikely comment that 'An arm of government may well decide to provide some form of help at the end of the day . . . I have not ruled out some long-term plans with either local or national government.' One 'arm of government' to which the Club appealed through Willie Whitelaw was the National Heritage Memorial Fund, although it is difficult to conceive how anyone can have thought a horserace came within its terms of reference.

A few weeks earlier at the All-Party Parliamentary Racing Committee, Clement Freud MP, ardent racegoer and owner of a hurdler, had suggested that the National Heritage Fund should step in, and Lord Charteris, Chairman of the Fund, had been consulted. Freud claimed that 'Aintree fits the bill and should be bought for the nation.' A more realistic comment was made by Lord Wigg, who said 'The purpose of the National Heritage Fund is not primarily the preservation of horseracing.'

Finally the Jockey Club took the bit between its teeth and called a press conference in London to announce its plans. Johnny Henderson said Davies was a 'tough negotiator' and this was too true as the Club had amazingly agreed to appeal for £7m. Privately, Henderson asked one of those helping with the Appeal 'Seven million is all right, isn't it?' and was told it was not. At this stage it was not supposed that the appeal could attain charitable status. Nevertheless a group consisting of Simon Weatherby, Henderson and Davies had met secretly at the Walton Group HQ on 19 March and agreed the £7m deal, and on 3 April, the day of the National, Henderson met Davies over a champagne breakfast at the Adelphi Hotel and signed the option.

12: Finding £7 Million

The retiring Senior Steward, Capt. John Macdonald-Buchanan, sat in his somewhat gloomy office overlooking Portman Square. High up in the building, with the square's tree-tops outside the window, the office should have been bright and redolent of the countryside, but it was not. Apart from a couple of pictures of horses, it was strictly functional. Macdonald-Buchanan was musing on the choice of people to run the Grand National campaign. Already he had come to the conclusion that John Derby must be the Chairman of the Appeal; it was not that the Club as a whole had a high opinion of John Derby, who had the appearance of one of the less energetic characters from a P. G. Wodehouse novel, but as Chairman he could be relied upon to be a figurehead who would not unduly interfere.

The money-raising aspect itself could be safely left, he thought, in the hands of Johnny Henderson. Henderson was immensely able, decisive and a partner in Cazenove & Co. He had been a member of the Club since 1965, a National Hunt man, and was already No. 2 at Ascot, working with the Queen's representative, John Abergavenny. At sixty-two Henderson was already running down his work in the City, and Macdonald-Buchanan thought he would be able to take on the Appeal without too much additional strain. What the Senior Steward did not take account of was that the Appeal required someone at the top with flair and *élan*, and Henderson's abilities were more pedestrian, in analysis and decision-making, as events were to show.

The lawyers had told the Jockey Club that they would require two trustees for the Appeal Fund, and Macdonald-Buchanan had concluded that while Lord Derby would be quite adequate as Chairman and trustee, he wanted someone less aristocratic, less obviously Jockey Club, as the other trustee. He had jotted down a list of several candidates. They were Lord Oaksey, Peter O'Sullevan, Michael Clayton, Maj. Tony Everett, Fred Winter and Chris Collins.

The first three were journalists, and on that account not entirely satisfactory, he thought, though they would undoubtedly help, which in fact they did. Everett was an owner who was keen to help the campaign, but he was not a well-known figure, unlike Fred Winter, one of the most renowned of trainers. But Macdonald-Buchanan doubted if Fred would take on the job in view of his heavy training schedule. Collins had favourable qualities, but it would be better to find a candidate who was not a member of the Jockey Club.

Following this line of thought, the Senior Steward settled on somebody who had not been on his initial list, Dick Francis, the ex-jockey and novelist. Early on, Francis had told the Club that he would do anything he could to help. As a noted rider of National Hunt horses he was an enthusiast, and he had subsequently achieved worldwide fame by successfully mixing crime and horseracing into a series of fictional plots which put him on the best-seller list. He was a modest, respectful man, who, to Macdonald-Buchanan's satisfaction, retained the jockey's traditional subservient stance when talking to the members of the Club.

Francis had a deep-rooted psychological connection with the National because in 1956 riding the Queen Mother's horse, Devon Loch, he had been well in the lead when the horse, to everyone's amazement, suddenly collapsed just a few yards short of the winning-post. Francis had to dismount and lead the horse in. No satisfactory reason was ever found for the horse's performance, although the Queen Mother, who was watching from the Royal Box, took a philosophic view. As a result, Francis had long felt a nagging sense of unhappiness about the National – he wrote, 'a post mortem would find the words Devon Loch engraved on my heart'. Now he wanted to do all he could to save it. It was soon settled that he and Lord Derby should be the joint trustees. Later, others were also asked to become trustees, among them Paul Mellon, the American millionaire and racecourse owner, and Councillor John Smith, the Liverpool personality and chairman of the city football club, who, it was thought, would focus Liverpool interests. But these trustees were in fact not formally appointed, and Derby and Francis alone became the trustees of the all-important charity when this too was formed.

The charitable connection began in this way. Johnny Henderson came to realize that raising such a large sum as Davies required was well beyond the capabilities of the Jockey Club alone. With Macdonald-Buchanan's agreement, Henderson decided that Lord Goodman, who was a member of the board of Racecourse Holdings Trust, should be approached to use his influence to see if the Appeal could be given charitable status.

It may seem extraordinary that it can ever have entered Henderson's mind that raising money to buy a horserace and a racecourse could be charitable. But the whole basis of British charitable law is quite extraordinary. As the Charity Law Reform Committee puts it, which of the following are charities? The United Nations Association, Amnesty, the Campaign against Racial Discrimination, the National Council for Civil Liberties. The answer is none! When the same question is asked of the following: Eton College, British Goat Society, Vegan Society, Reading Temperance Society, British Society of Dowsers and the Lord's Day Observance Society, the answer is that all are charities.

So if Eton College (which seventy-five per cent of the Jockey Club attended) can be a charity, why should the Grand National not be likewise? Equally, it may seem strange that Lord Goodman could help bring this about, although not so curious when it is remembered that he is probably the number one name on what *The Times* calls 'the famous list of the Good and the Great' and has been so since the 1950s when the Treasury department that kept it was actually called 'G and G'. *The Times* says that the 'phrase has always had a pompous faintly risible ring about it'. 'These days the list is a very swish affair, all floppy discs and visual display terminals, run by a staff of nine and lubricated by a budget of £250,000 a year.' Furthermore, Lord Goodman, or 'The Blessed Arnold' as *Private Eye* calls him, had been the chairman of a noted report on charity law which had stated that although there are many different privileges accorded to charities 'the financial privileges are now of the greatest significance. Although the smaller organizations may lack the large incomes and endowments of big charities, they are nevertheless often dependent on gaining charitable status, as such status is almost always the prerequisite grant aid from charitable trusts.' Most members of the Jockey Club were, be it remembered, also involved in family or business charitable trusts.

So Henderson set about persuading Goodman to talk to the Charity Commission about an acceptable proposal for Aintree. Goodman, in his report a few years earlier, had said of sport that 'the encouragement of sport and recreation should be recognized as an independent and charitable object provided the necessary elements of altruism and benefit to a sufficient section of the community are present'. The Charity Commissioners did not consider that the Aintree Racecourse and the Grand National had the necessary elements of altruism, and it was therefore vital to find some other route. It looked as if this could be in the area covered by the Recreational Charities Act of 1958 which said that 'it shall be and deemed always to have been charitable to provide or assist in the provision of facilities for recreation or other leisure time occupation, if the facilities are provided in the interests of social welfare'. Goodman suggested that if 100 acres in the middle of the racecourse were set aside for recreational purposes, then this could be a charitable object.

The charitable laws are sufficiently flexible that it was not even necessary to define precisely where the 100 acres should be. If the Charity Commissioners are presented with a model trust document which meets all their requirements, then the whole process of granting status can take as little as ten days, in contrast to the position when there are doubts, and it may take a year. With Lord Goodman's help, the Grand National's approval went through very quickly indeed.

At the news, joy was unconfined in the corridors of the Jockey Club. After all, most of the members had trusts of one kind or another. There was the Leverhulme Charitable Trust, the Wates

Foundation, the Simon Marks Trust, the Weinstock Fund, the de Rothschild Charitable Settlement, and many others. All of them knew, intimately, about charities. Take Lord Huntington, son and heir to the Duke of Devonshire, who had been interviewed on the subject by a witty writer on *The Times*, at the family seat, Chatsworth, whose 'ownership reposed today in various charitable trusts. His family occupied only a small part of the house. "We pay rent," said Lord Hartington. "Furnished rooms!"'

It did not occur to such men that by contributing to the purchase of 100 acres for the recreational needs of Liverpudlians they would not be contributing to the acquisition of the Grand National, except obliquely. They saw it as their traditional means of enabling the rich to make grand gestures of giving, making their kind richer, and yet remaining nearly as rich as before. They had always done it that way and they were to do it again.

One small drawback was the fiscal limit to the amount of charity-giving to be allowed. On the basis that the purchase of the racecourse might be valued at £5m, the Charity Commissioners set the value of the mysterious 100 acres, on a *pro rata* basis, at just under £2m, and this was to be the limit of charitable giving. If more was given to the charity, there would have to be further discussion with the Commissioners.

In blissful ignorance of the problems posed by the charity sector of the Appeal, Lord Derby and Dick Francis were opted as trustees, but the onerous responsibilities that office implied were not explained to them, nor did they know what a tangled web was being woven.

13: A New Target

Because such a large number of Jockey Club members were either anti-National, or anti-Bill Davies, the Senior Steward decided it would be politic to make the Appeal pay its own way in every respect. All facilities in the way of office accommodation, equipment, telephones, even copying, were to be paid for. So was secretarial and other assistance.

The question was, where was the money to come from? It was not possible to use money collected for the Fund to pay for these administrative expenses. For one thing, the Trust deed required that if the Appeal failed, all sums of £5 or over should be returned to the donors. Sums under £5 could be retained, it is true, but in total they would amount to very little. The interest on the capital donated could be retained, but this again did not amount to much in the early days of the campaign. If the Appeal succeeded, it would be possible to pay off the expenses, but some of these, notably the legal charges, would be very heavy indeed.

Simon Weatherby, Secretary to the Jockey Club, got in touch with Lord Derby and explained the position. He would have to find a way of collecting a sum to pay the expenses of setting up the office, preferably by canvassing other Club members, and Simon suggested the figure of £100,000. Derby checked through the list of members, but did not choose very wisely and, further-more, wrote a somewhat less than tactful letter explaining what was wanted. He indicated that £5,000 each was required – he wrote to about twenty members – and suggested that the money might be repaid if the Appeal succeeded. The result was disappointing. The Jockey Club membership, far from planning to buy Aintree, were very reluctant to put up £5,000 apiece to encourage others to do so on their behalf.

The reasons they gave were many and various. One (described in the press as a millionaire) said he just couldn't find £5,000 – or any lesser sum – as he was investing everything in a new business venture. Another wrote to Derby with a most elaborate rationale, reached he said after much heart-searching. He told Derby that the National is not the race it was when we were young; it was pansy now, won by very moderate horses. Again, and perhaps a contradiction, owners are not prepared to run the risk of taking on the National with its great hazards and so many starters . . . Finally, he did not think the Club would raise the necessary amount of money . . . the average racegoer will merely say 'Well if the Jockey Club wants to save the Grand National, it is a body with a great many very rich men in it and why don't they put up the cash?' This was very true, but hardly a reason for declining to part with £5,000. Another refusal letter from a peer said the Club was allowing itself to be blackmailed by unscrupulous property developers and he would like to see the present deal cancelled. 'Sorry to be beastly,' he added.

In the end, by pushing some ditherers, it was possible to attract money from about a dozen members (and remember this was for a modest £5,000 each) and on this basis a simple office was set up in Portman Square. A small staff of enthusiasts moved in, but the watchword was economy, and they were encouraged to work on ideas that would cost nothing to introduce. They came up with a strange medley of proposals. One was to write begging letters to every MFH, but the hunts had problems of their own. Another was to persuade Dick Francis to sign his books, but how would this bring in funds? Then lists were produced of all the celebrities who had racing interests, so that approaches could be made to Penelope Keith the actress, pop stars Chas and Dave, Mel Smith and Anthony Andrews. Among other names which were conjured up were Jimmy Hill the commentator, Terry Wogan the broadcaster and Elizabeth Taylor the film star, then visiting England, who had been the star of *National Velvet*, and might help. A memo was written proposing the mass-production of car stickers for sale at hunts, racecourses, shows and so on, selling at £1 each and reading 'I'm helping to save the Grand National – are you?' An advertisement headed 'Save the National!' appeared in some of the sporting journals but since it asked for money to be sent direct to the Appeal's bank account, there was no way of knowing if it produced any result. The bank account took in a few pounds day by day, usually accompanied by enthusiastic letters from the public.

The Appeal also attracted attention from various commercial organizations who presented themselves as well-wishers who would benefit the National without themselves being much out of pocket. One such concern had purchased Miss Topham's Rolls-Royce and offered to drive it to racecourses to collect donations, from which expenses would be deducted. Another was the family Rougier which had purchased the famous horse Red Rum, and made a living by personal appearances. Indeed, Red Rum has earned more from commercial events than he did from prize money. There were T-shirt manufacturers, tie manufacturers, badge manufacturers and sporting artists and sculptors. All would help by selling their wares, they said.

While these various offers were being analysed and considered, the Grand National race itself came and went. The Appeal office had had plans for collecting money at the National, but after endless discussion, nothing was done. The race itself was particularly exciting. Grittar won, and Dick Saunders, the oldest rider ever to win the National, hung up his boots.

The only cloud which fell over this joyous National was the criticism which spread quickly regarding the Appeal in general and the Jockey Club in particular. Why had they not taken the opportunity to acquaint the great British public with what was happening? Why had there not been collecting tins on hand for the benefit of the punters on the course? One sporting paper suggested that at least £1m might have been collected in this way. And why had there not been leaflets telling the public what was going on? Where should they send their cheques? It was monstrous that the public remained in ignorance about how to donate to the Appeal, said the press.

Stung to the depths by this criticism, which was widespread, the Appeal office decided that in future they would not be vulnerable, and they set about ordering several dozen plastic collecting tins. When they enquired about the legal mechanics of employing collecting tins, the problem was more complex. Each collector, with his tin, had to be an official of the Appeal, or at least have a letter of authorization. It would not be legal to put tins in betting shops. Nevertheless such niceties could sometimes be overcome, and when the Badminton Horse Trials opened in April, several members of the office arranged to mingle with the huge crowd gathered at the Duke of Beaufort's estate. Hour after hour they went round the course, rattling their tins. Finally, they sat down and emptied them. The result – £12.56. It was an object lesson, and they did not again try a direct money-raising appeal without more careful planning.

Over Easter, at his country house at Lower Swell in the Cotswolds, Capt. Macdonald-Buchanan, the Senior Steward, pondered on the position and took stock. He was a decisive thinker, and he summed up the Appeal in one word. It was a flop. A few thousand pounds had been donated, but in the Jockey Club itself there was a distinct air of apathy. Following the usual procedure there of putting each activity under a Steward (these were the eight 'prefects' or 'directors') Capt. Macdonald-Buchanan decided that the time had come to allocate a Steward to the Appeal, and the man he chose was Sam Vestey. He wrote asking him to manage the campaign. This would not mean ousting John Derby – merely pushing him to one side – since he would retain the title of Chairman and would not have anything to do with day-to-day fund raising. Henderson would continue to work with Vestey, specializing on the legal and financial aspects.

Sam Vestey was in the habit of calling regularly at the Jockey Club on Monday mornings as he was driven from Paddington station after a weekend at his Gloucestershire home; Portman Square lay on the route to his office at Smithfield meat market. After receiving the Senior Steward's letter he called in to see Macdonald-Buchanan and together they mapped out a quick strategy. First, scrap most of the Appeal office staff and call in professionals. Second, negotiate with Davies to reduce the option price well below the £7m figure. Third, be more outspoken with the press and public.

Sam was not a man to let the grass grow under his feet. He saw here an opportunity to make his mark in the Jockey Club. He could do something for the country as a whole, and so expunge from the record the unwelcome reputation he had acquired as a result of the newspaper campaign against the Vestey family's tax record. He could show that he was, clearly, public spirited. Within days, he was getting together a new team, centred round a professional group of fund-raisers headed by an American, which put an executive into the Portman Square office at a fee of £3,650 a month.

Despite the Senior Steward's diplomacy, Lord Derby was not particularly pleased to have been edged off the centre of the Grand National stage. He therefore arranged a re-entry which, he thought, would push him back in front of the footlights. Early in May he chaired a meeting of the twenty-six-strong Steering Committee in one of the dismal rooms which the Jockey Club rented for such purposes from the Brewers' Society. Before the meeting, he had privately informed Vestey and the Senior Steward of the news he had acquired, or, as he described it, the bombshell he was to drop. Now, facing the meeting, which included two journalists, Oaksey and O'Sullevan, he swore them all to the greatest confidentiality, and announced that the Merseyside Councy Council had decided to place a compulsory purchase order on Aintree. Obviously, he said, it was no longer necessary for the Jockey Club to raise £7m and the Appeal would have to be deferred.

There was general agreement all round the table, because the members saw at once that it might be possible this way to buy Aintree for as little as £1m, the value of the agricultural land. This would be a great coup. Henderson made the point that Davies could not for a moment be allowed to believe that there had been collusion between the Jockey Club and the Merseyside Council, so Derby proposed that the Falkland War Appeal, just launched, must take priority with the public, and the National Appeal deferred until it was over. It was unsaid, but understood, that the Appeal could thus go into a state of suspended animation on this pretext, while in fact waiting for Merseyside to act, and without there being any suggestion that the Club knew what the Council was up to.

In fact, the Merseyside County Council's plan was somewhat ill-considered, as we shall see.

To keep the public quiet, the Club had put out a press release listing the membership of the Steering Committee; the *Sporting*

Chronicle commented 'Some of the members . . . found themselves on the Committee without having actually agreed to
serve.' They would do their bit, said the paper, if the Jockey Club
would only tell them what that bit was.

Two weeks later, Derby again came down from Liverpool to
attend another meeting of the Steering Committee. As usual he
stayed at Claridge's, which was within walking distance of
Portman Square, so after breakfast he paid a call on the Senior
Steward, only to find the whole Merseyside proposal less popular
in the Club than it had been during the euphoria of the earlier
meeting. It seemed that the Council had decided that it could not
go ahead with a compulsory purchase order which put a burden
on the ratepayers of Liverpool, a body which, with one of the
highest unemployment rates in Europe to support, had other
priorities than a racecourse. So Raymond O'Brien, the leader of
the Council, conceived the idea of approaching the Levy Board
for a handout, or at any rate asking them to guarantee the cost of
the purchase. The Club did not particularly like the idea of the
Levy Board controlling Aintree, although it would not have
objected to a guarantee.

So the Senior Steward and some of his officials together with
Derby, quickly convened a meeting to discuss the matter with
Chris Collins and Gen. Sir Cecil ('Monkey') Blacker MC, the
Jockey Club's representative on the Levy Board. 'Monkey'
Blacker had a close connection with Aintree described in his
book *A Soldier in the Saddle*. In it, he tells how 'my second life
was lived in the world of steeplechasing . . . Fortunately I had
saved up my pay during the war for just this moment, and I was
able to buy a steeplechaser of my own . . . I was determined to
ride in the National one day' (he did, so did his son) but he
described how he was able to enter a lesser steeplechase at
Aintree, and fell at the fence before Becher's. As he walked
away, he found his horse was being held by a spectator, a professional jockey, who told him 'Everyone else is down – jump on
and finish the course and the race is yours.' The crowd around
him were reminiscent of a boxing crowd urging the smaller man
to go in and fight. Eventually be decided to go, and won – as he
thought – only to find that another rider had done the same thing
before him, so he was only second.

To return to the meeting, 'Monkey' Blacker gave a spirited

account of the attitude of the various factions on the Levy Board, including that of Lord Plummer, now about to retire, summing up by giving it as his view that the Levy Board would not back the Merseyside County Council. He was right; they would not. After this meeting, the Board agreed unanimously that it would not wish to be associated with the promotion of such legislation. The Board was also faced with the further complication that, as the price would not be known in advance, it would be required to enter into a binding financial commitment, which although capable of informed assessment, would in fact be unspecific. The Board considered this could not be recommended to the Home Office for approval.

This put O'Brien and the Council, and Lord Derby, in a quandary because it meant that funds would have to be found elsewhere, and furthermore the Home Office had tipped off O'Brien that a compulsory purchase order would be most unlikely to have government approval – after all it was a Conservative government. Finally, if the order were to succeed, it would have to go the private members' route through Parliament. Derby asked for the views of Sir Timothy Kitson MP, a member of the Steering Committee and joint-chairman of the All-Party Parliamentary Racing Group who said that a more favourable procedure would be to raise the matter in the House of Lords, but it would take months or years to go through. Lord Derby was despondent.

It is difficult to assess how far the Merseyside County Council in general, and O'Brien, its publicity-conscious leader, were serious about all this, and how far they were using the threat of an order to lever Davies into the arms of the Jockey Club. Davies himself never succeeded in finding out, and although he paid several visits to the Council, he was left with the impression that they would pursue the compulsory purchase order if all else failed, because Aintree was an essential attraction to Liverpool and must not disappear. At this early stage the public knew little of this, but after the meeting of the Steering Committee, the Jockey Club put out another uninformative statement about the Appeal which mentioned in passing that a local Aintree council (not Merseyside) wished to put Aintree in a Green Belt area. Derby said privately that he did not think a Green Belt designation for Aintree would go through.

About this time there was another change in the personalities at the Jockey Club, which had its effect on the conduct of negotiations, brought about by the routine election of Lord Rupert Manton as Senior Steward in place of the retiring Macdonald-Buchanan. The two men could hardly have been less alike. The retiring Senior Steward was extrovert, amusing, forceful and crisp in his comments on the business in hand. Manton was reserved, dry, and had that typical upper-class characteristic of speaking through clenched teeth in a quiet staccato tone. He was also the unfortunate recipient of critical comments in *Private Eye* one of which is quoted in his biography. It also claimed he was known as 'Soapy' but of course in the corridors of Portman Square he was invariably known as 'Senior Steward' and never as Lord Manton.

He was quoted in the *Tatler* as saying that he would have to spend more time in Portman Square (actually he was at home or at the races for a major part of the week) because 'We've got to get more involved in the corridors of power. Try to persuade the government that they are taking too much out of the sport.' The *Tatler* added that softening up ministers with jaunts to the race-courses and plenty of agreeable claret was now high on the Steward's agenda.

Whether for this or for other reasons, Manton took less than an active part in the activities of the Appeal compared with his predecessor who had worked very hard to get it on the rails. Indeed, Manton left Sam Vestey to dash ahead with various schemes for raising money, without, at this stage, actually raising any, and one of his first targets was the Americans.

Racing people who supported the National put great faith in the prospect of the Americans coming to its rescue. After all, Paul Mellon, one of the richest men in America, and Raymond Guest, a former US Ambassador to Ireland, were honorary members of the Jockey Club. Mellon had agreed to be a patron in view of his ardent interest in steeplechasing, and of his ownership of Mill Reef, among the most famous horses ever to win the Derby. Yet when Vestey talked privately with him during one of the American's visits to England during the summer, he did not get the impression that a very large sum would be forthcoming. Vestey knew that steeplechasing is very much the poor relation to flat racing in America, and races are rare, as punters do not like the risks associated with horses that might fall. Prize money is nevertheless grandiose by English standards, and in addition to Mellon some very rich people supported jumping.

In the circumstances it seemed right to mount a vigorous campaign in the USA, using Mellon's name, but masterminded by someone with a definite commitment, and Vestey was convinced the appropriate man was Charlie Fenwick (pronounced Fen-wick) who had ridden twice in the Grand National, and in 1980 had won at the second attempt, riding his father-in-law's horse Ben Nevis. Fenwick had stayed with the family of Sam Vestey's new wife during the winter of 1980 when he was training for the race, so there was a personal as well as a sporting connection.

Vestey asked for a meeting with Fenwick, and this turned out to be possible only by sandwiching it between various appointments during one of Fenwick's visits to London – he was a banker with some international business. So Vestey, his wife Celia, the fund-raisers and Fenwick met in a private room at Brown's Hotel on 25 June. Vestey outlined the plan for the appeal and Fenwick agreed to head it up. A video set was dragged into the room, and Vestey showed Fenwick the half-hour video which had been made by Ivor Herbert, a sporting journalist, and paid for by the Levy Board. This was, at that time, the Levy Board's sole contribution to the Grand National Appeal (although they were soon to lend the Jockey Club £250,000, repayable later) and it was somewhat strange that it should be for a video aimed at the American market only, with very little interest to UK audiences. Fenwick remarked that he liked the content and would like it still more when it had the promised introduction by Prince Charles.

Over breakfast, Fenwick got out his diary and said that most of the steeplechasing fraternity of America would be assembling at Saratoga racecourse early in August and he thought Vestey should be there to talk to them. Sam readily agreed. It was understood that in the month ahead, all the paperwork would be prepared so that potential American donors could be approached at Saratoga or immediately afterwards. Fenwick was charmed with all this and pleased to meet the new Lady Vestey again, and glad to be involved with the British racing scene once more.

On his return to the States he phoned to say that the visit ought to be made not by Vestey alone but by several famous British trainers and jockeys as well – he mentioned Bruce Hobbs, who as a seventeen-year-old had ridden Battleship to victory in the National for an American owner; Dick Saunders, the oldest man ever to win; Fred Winter and Fulke Walwyn, who had both ridden and trained a winner. In the event, only four were able to go: Vestey, Fred Winter, Dick Saunders and Lord (John) Oaksey, who wrote for the *Daily Telegraph* under the name 'Marlborough', and had ridden in the race. There was some consternation at the thought that the Appeal would have to pay for four North Atlantic fares, and a secretary was despatched from the Appeal office to visit all the bucket-shops in the locality to obtain the keenest-priced ticket.

In the tree-lined paddock of Saratoga, oldest and loveliest racecourse in the United States, the four visitors met their American friends, including many who owned or had owned jumpers in the UK, notably Mrs Marion du Pont who won the National with Battleship in 1938. The other living American winner (besides Fenwick) Tommy Smith was there, together with others who had competed at Aintree like George Strawbridge, Gene Weymouth and Tim Durant, probably the oldest man ever to complete the course at Liverpool. Also present was American George Sloan who accomplished the extraordinary feat of becoming the British amateur jockeys' champion in the 1977/8 season. George owns health spas in Nashville, trains his own horses there and runs the Hillsboro Foxhounds from his 1,400-acre estate. Lord Oaksey described Saratoga as 'an extraordinary phenomenon', a town which sleeps for eleven months of the year and comes alive for the twelfth, a hectic circus revolving around the track and the sales.

'The wide streets of elegant nineteenth-century houses are much as they were when racing came here first in 1860. Many of the houses are lovely, but a few need only several bats and a couple of monsters to put them straight back into a Charles Adams cartoon. As someone said proudly "things are nice and informal here, you can get kicked by all the best horses".'

Oaksey added that 'as we met and talked after racing that evening, in the ring where millions of dollars will change hands at this year's Yearling Sales, there was no mistaking the enthusiasm which a small but extremely rich and influential group of Americans still feel for British jumping in general and the

National in particular'. Oaksey went on to affirm that we 'did not have our begging bowls with us and brought back no blank cheques'. The US campaign was now being advised by an extremely high-powered firm of American lawyers, he said, and 'my confident guess is that with their help Charlie Fenwick will be able to draw up a scheme based probably on some form of limited partnership'. 'Many of those we met were perfectly prepared to make straight no-string donations, simply to preserve something they think worth preserving.' Oaksey went on to claim that if US donors got something in return, the UK would have to do likewise, but the campaign committee 'is not agreed' on a form of shareholding.

Oaksey concluded: 'No doubt it was all too easy to feel optimistic – cushioned and lubricated at Saratoga by the unbelievable hospitality for which the Americans are famous. As we sat in the sales arena for instance, an amazing collection of originals by Munnings glowed around the walls. They will be for sale with the yearlings – and the combined proceeds would undoubtedly buy half a dozen Aintrees.'

He also mentioned that the mission, beautifully organized as it was by Charlie Fenwick, had to be rushed and was insufficiently prepared. As we shall see, Vestey came to believe this also. The major problem was not in fact one of organization at all, it was that Fenwick now realized that the rich US enthusiasts wished to donate money in the way they always donated money, and in no other way – and that was by giving to an American charity. A British charity (and that existed thanks to Lord Goodman) was alas useless, because it would have not produced tax advantages for the US citizen. At first this seemed an insuperable obstacle, but Fenwick's 'high-powered' lawyers soon came upon a possible vehicle in the form of a US entity called Royal Oak Trust, which was the American arm for collecting funds for the National Trust.

By 15 September, negotiations with them had already reached an advanced stage, and a Mr Arthur Prager, the new director of the Royal Oak Foundation, who was in England making a tour of National Trust properties, visited the Jockey Club and met Vestey. He explained to him that many rich Americans liked to give to the National Trust houses – for example one was currently giving furniture to Igtham Mote in Kent – and the money for this was currently collected by Royal Oak who, after a deduction, passed the funds on to the National Trust. The US Revenue authorities would, Mr Prager thought, look more favourably on Royal Oak if it also acted as a vehicle for other British charities. He thought it likely that his board would consider their acting for the Grand National, charging a fee which would be between ten and fifteen per cent of the donations received.

Despite all this, Vestey thought the American venture had been a disaster. He complained that he was pushed into such activities far too early. He called it 'highly embarrassing' that he hadn't been able to tell the Americans how much money he wanted. Yet Fenwick, who was also cautious, was now talking in terms of raising $1m, if the Royal Oak position could be resolved. The fact was that by now Vestey had come to the conclusion that the Appeal could only raise about half the £7m that Davies had asked for his option. The professional fund-raisers were also aghast at the task facing them, which would have involved collecting over £1m a month to 1 November. The atmosphere was all wrong and the time of the year was inappropriate. They drew up a chart which analysed all the actions required to raise funds and at the head they wrote 'Decide the £ need'. So it came about that Vestey set himself the task of negotiating with Davies a new '£ need' well below the £7m figure.

While the negotiations with Davies were continuing, Vestey was adamant that there should be no meetings or proposals put to any overseas interests. This decision set back the Appeal significantly, even in quite minor ways. For example the video film which the Levy Board had financed was to have an introduction and conclusion by Prince Charles, who long before had offered to do whatever he could to assist the race. Vestey, who played polo with the Prince, refused point blank to ask him to make the film until the negotiations were complete. On one occasion he said he had been dining the night before with Prince Charles who had asked to see the film 'but I refused to show it to him'.

More significant aspects of the Appeal which were delayed while the negotiations continued concerned the contribution to be made by the Irish, the French, the Australians, Hong Kong and the Arabs. Early on in the campaign Vestey had been in touch with Joseph McGrath, a steward of the Turf Club of

Ireland, and he was full of enthusiasm, confident that the Irish would contribute in a substantial way. Later Jonathan Irwin of Goff's arranged a lunch for some twenty leading figures in Irish racing, but their conclusion was that it would be wrong to put anything in motion until the negotiations with Davies were concluded. Sam Vestey visited Ireland again where, said *Horse and Hound*, he was well received. As might be expected there were some dissenting voices at helping the fund, based on the fact that some Irish horses had been balloted out last year after travelling to Liverpool to run.

No approaches were made to other national bodies except for informal talks at Hong Kong, where it was made clear that no cash of significance would be forthcoming, and a visit to Australia by Lord Derby was also unfruitful.

The Arabs were, everyone agreed, a different matter. They were described by the fund-raisers as a special and very rich sub-group of owners and Vestey had his own way of looking at them when he told the astonished fund-raisers that 'their [i.e. the Arabs'] view of money is quite different from yours and mine'.

The Jockey Club's relations with Arab owners had been curious for some time. It was generally said – indeed publicly said in the press – that the Club ought to elect some of the more successful Arabs to membership. This had gone so far, rumour went, that the Club indicated to the Aga Khan that he would be elected if he so chose. However just at this time there was an unfortunate incident when his horse was suspected of being doped, and such was the power of the Jockey Club that it was said that the Aga Khan contacted the Club to say that as he was suspected of doping he must withdraw his application for membership, and concurrently he spent a small fortune on chemical tests which established that his horse had manufactured its own drug. Whether these rumours were true or not, neither the Aga Khan nor any of the other rich Eastern owners were in fact elected to membership. Other methods of establishing some relationship between Arab owners and the Club were examined, but nothing came of them.

So the Club was ambivalent in its attitude to the Arab owners, and while it prepared lists of their names, their addresses and titles, their trainers, their jockeys, their friends and relations, only the most tentative feelers were put out to those who might have, it was thought, useful connections with them. The received opinion about the Arab owners was that they all had flats in Belgravia and were devoted to flat racing alone. Bucking this trend was a Saudi tycoon with a pad in Somerset within spitting distance of Glastonbury and with an undying devotion to steeple-chasing. He told *The Sunday Times*, 'Jumping is a beautiful sport. So we want to get interested and we do not do too bad.' The tycoon, Sheikh Ali Aba Khamsin, trained as a civil engineer, decided to take horse ownership seriously in 1979 and accord-ingly paid a visit to the famous Fred Winter. 'I drove to see Mr Winter myself. He agreed to help me. We fixed a budget.' But like all steeplechase owners, the expenses of his twenty-five horses still exceed their winnings. When Mr Winter privately sounded him about the possibility of a contribution to the Grand National Appeal, the answer was not encouraging.

So it was that only sporadic progress was made in the late summer with the groups that were in the earlier halcyon days expected to be among the most generous of donors. No specific expectations could be counted on from the Arabs, from Australia or from Liverpool.

Another area of expectation was the City. In July Henderson had chaired a meeting with a small group of interested people but nothing further was done until the early autumn when Hon. David Montagu, a banker, met with a small group at the Turf Club, and over several bottles of champagne, set about dis-cussing how the City might help. It was soon clear that whatever form their help might take, it would not consist of putting many individual hands in individual pockets. Ideas were floated, such as approaching big advertisers to sponsor jumps at the National. Montagu thought that the multinational companies would be interested in the overseas coverage of the race, but it is probable that he was misinformed, because as we shall see no such adver-tising proposals were ever put to the test. Another proposal discussed was Henderson's idea that there should be an auction, possibly held in conjunction with Whitbreads, who had offered a free dinner in their brewery premises in lieu of a donation. This somewhat clashed with the offer of a prominent Jockey Club member to give bottles of wine from his wine business for a special dinner for donors again in lieu of a donation. It was decided to pursue all these various entertaining ideas, much to the chagrin of the fund-raisers, who had hoped that, at some point, money was going to be mentioned.

These schemes would all have to be brought face to face with reality, but that could not happen until a deal with Davies was finalized. In the meantime the horsey world discussed endlessly how easy or difficult it would be to achieve a multimillion-pound racing certainty.

14: Getting the Better of Davies

The Jockey Club publicized its negotiating position in a most unusual way by arranging for its press office to send out a document which began 'This is *not* a press statement, but a paper clarifying various points.' It was headed 'For information only'. This unusual, not to say, naïve, technique of sending the press information which was not a press statement, caused considerable bewilderment. For example the *Sporting Chronicle* wrote: 'We had that strange and disturbing paper from Lord Derby which refuted most of the important points we thought had been agreed, but did little to clarify the real state of negotiations with Davies.' This referred to the first three points of the paper, which said:

(1) The Jockey Club has *not* offered to pay £7m to the Walton Commercial Group to purchase the course.
(2) The correct situation is that the Jockey Club have negotiated a legally binding option to purchase the course, exercisable by the Trustees at any time up until 1 November 1982.
(3) The figure of £7m is the value put on this option by Mr Davies.

The point being made was that Sam Vestey needed to talk to Davies about a new option to include agreement on the 1983 race. The press began to suspect this, but in fact nothing much happened until a middleman appeared who was dramatically to change the course of events.

It was in mid-August, and Vestey was being driven from his Eaton Mews flat to the office, when he took a call on his car telephone from a *Sporting Life* journalist whom he admired, John McCririck. The journalist said that he had been asked by Davies, whom he knew well, to act as a go-between, McCririck having mentioned that he and Vestey got on well together. It was true that relationships between sporting journalists and leading racing personalities tended to be close because they met so frequently at race meetings that there was little formality in the encounter. Many of the journalists had been to the right schools; McCririck was a Harrovian. He was a colourful character, not only in his hirsute appearance, but in the choice of clothes which he wore on the race-track as well as on the dog-track to which he was much attached.

Without delay, it was arranged to meet in Vestey's office where McCririck made it clear that Davies wanted at least £4¾m. This was the figure he had arrived at after a successful negotiation with his banks, but he felt sure they would not accept anything less now than a guaranteed certainty, and promises alone from the Jockey Club would not suffice. After a few talks McCririck and Davies came to trust Vestey implicitly and felt sure they could reach a deal very close to the desired figure. Davies and Vestey were quickly on Christian-name terms, but this in fact meant very little, because Sam Vestey always urged those around him to use his Christian name, and it was rare to hear anyone m'lording him.

Meanwhile Johnny Henderson was in contact with United Dominions Trust, Davies's lead bank, hoping to convince them that only £4m was available. The alternative facing the banks was to put Davies into liquidation, with all the inevitable delays in getting their money that would result.

Early in September, Simon Weatherby, Secretary to the Jockey Club, who was playing an increasing role in the negotiations, drafted a letter for Lord Derby to sign, which spelt out quite clearly to Davies that the Club's limit was £4m – and even that could not be certain of achievement. He added that Racecouse Holdings Trust (the Jockey Club subsidiary) would be prepared to pay £¼m for the benefit of running the 1983 race (this being the anticipated profit if £200,000 or so was received for the TV rights). Derby signed the letter and off it went.

This letter was to throw Davies into a violent rage, but strangely enough its arrival at his office coincided with a totally false story in a Liverpool paper, probably based on a tip from Davies's office, asserting that the 'National is Saved'. The writer claimed a deal had been signed two days before, and that Davies would 'get his cash' on 1 November from the Jockey Club 'who have coughed up the cash out of their own pockets'. None of this was true, although the journalist persisted in repeating it on the BBC lunch-time news, much to the confusion of the racing fraternity.

To return to Davies and the go-between McCririck, the latter telephoned Vestey to say how angry had been the scene on receipt of the Derby letter. Davies was convinced Vestey had offered him £4¾m, not £4m, and McCririck later said that in taking their stand on the smaller figure, the Jockey Club in fact compromised their own negotiator, Lord Vestey. 'In my presence he has consistently offered more,' he said. For his part, Vestey denied that he had ever offered £4¾m.

Davies, now thoroughly disillusioned, wanted to have a contract from the Jockey Club for the full amount. The same night he rang Vestey twice at his country house, Stowell Park, talking each time for half an hour or more, and reiterating that he wanted a contract and the interest paid on any money outstanding. Vestey told him that this was impossible; the Jockey Club would not sign a contract to pay the money, and it would be impossible to find interest payments for a sum still to be collected. As events were to show, the money was collected very slowly indeed, so the interest payments, had they been promised, would have been penal.

At this point in the negotiations, Vestey was careful to check his position with the Jockey Club, first with Simon Weatherby, who was adamant about the limit being £4m. He added that there was no question of the Club handing over money now; it had no money. Johnny Henderson too was consulted, and he also urged 'we must stand firm at £4m' because Davies would 'come to heel'.

For his part, Davies had now lost faith in Vestey, believing that he did not have authority to speak for the Jockey Club, although he made one last attempt to contact him, in early October, but Vestey was on holiday in Scotland, shooting and fishing. On the Sunday, Davies phoned Henderson, just as the latter was leaving his Newbury house for church, and reiterated his proposals, which he added would also be acceptable to United Dominions Trust. Henderson told him that the Derby letter was not negotiable and was surprised when Davies said he could not take this seriously as Vestey had told him to disregard the letter. Henderson could not believe this.

On the following day, Davies sent his assistant, Sue Sadler, to London to visit Simon Weatherby, bearing with her three typed agreements between his company and the Jockey Club. They incorporated the requests Davies had already made. Simon said he could not sign the documents, and reiterated that no guarantees could be given, although he would look over the papers and send a formal letter rejecting the proposal, which he did on 7 October. Both Sue and McCririck telephoned Simon to check if his letter really represented the Jockey Club's position. McCririck said that if so, Davies was seriously reconsidering where he stood, this being the first time that Davies had really appreciated that perhaps £4¾m was not obtainable. Sue Sadler said that she and McCririck would have to spend the weekend convincing Davies that £4m was the limit.

Despite the fact that his kidney illness was visibly weakening Simon Weatherby day by day, and he was spending more and more time on his machine, no one could have been more dedicated to the intricacies of the Appeal than he was. Three months later, Simon Weatherby would be dead, yet now he struggled to untie the tangled knot which Davies was ravelling, while at the same time exhibiting a toughness as a negotiator which was unrivalled in the Club, based on an intellectual appreciation of the position, which could be summed up in the phrase 'Davies has nowhere else to turn'.

Over that weekend, at home in Gloucestershire, Simon Weatherby spent a considerable amount of time on the telephone talking to McCririck and Sue Sadler and when he returned to Portman Square he was convinced that Davies had not given up hope of getting £4¾m. Vestey also talked to Davies, and discussed the possibility of a meeting, but at 5 p.m. Sue phoned to say no meeting was possible and a joint statement should be issued to say talks had broken down over the matter of the guarantee. The following day Collins visited Aintree to talk to the staff about the future, but Davies declined to see him.

It therefore came as no surprise to the Club that on 13 October McCririck published a story in *Sporting Life* headlined 'Next year's Grand National looks a non-starter. Aintree deal falls down, miracle is needed now.' In the story, Davies made a bitter attack on the Jockey Club – he accused them of being 'determined to screw him into the ground'. Davies asked 'What happens when they come back next May and say they've only managed to raise £1m? Will they want yet another option?' This was an all-too-realistic worry, because exactly such a scenario was discussed on several occasions in Portman Square, and just as hurriedly pushed aside as not to be contemplated. Davies went on, 'It's absurd for them to say they haven't got £4m [to guarantee]. They are some of the wealthiest men in Britain and if they just underwrote that amount, that would be enough for my bankers. They either want to save Aintree or they don't.' The paper added that 'he is convinced the Club is gambling on the course falling into their laps in a year or two'.

McCririck described how as a go-between for two parties who have no mutual respect and continually attribute the basest of motives to each other, he had been 'on the butt end of their adverse comments about each other which . . . blighted all negotiations'. He added 'Can't all those involved, even now, realize that the world's greatest horserace deserves better than this?'

The next day, the Jockey Club held one of its rare meetings at the Newmarket headquarters of the Club, and Vestey got to his feet to tell the assembled members what was happening to the National. When he had finished, and the members realized that negotiations might break down for failure to find a guarantee, there was some gloom. One member, called Phillips, stood up to propose that the members should each guarantee £50,000 and offered to do so himself. Vestey answered him, but politely brushed his proposal aside, so that it was never followed up. The fact was that most members of the Club did not want to give personal guarantees of any kind.

Early the following morning, Sam Vestey drove down to the helicopter take-off pad by Blackfriars Bridge and boarded his 'chopper' to fly to the races. At the meeting, he told friends that he was desperately trying to put together a package, because the Club was the only interested buyer. It was 'difficult' though to guarantee the money when the campaign had hardly started.

In short, the Jockey Club closed ranks and waited for Davies to give in. But it then turned out that it was not only Davies who had to give in, but his banks as well.

Davies, who had nowhere else to turn, was having some difficulty in persuading his banks to agree to the Jockey Club proposal. It was unattractive to the banks, because there was no guarantee that £4m would be raised and Davies himself had already been quoted as saying 'What happens when they come back next May and say they've only managed to raise £1m?' The banks would therefore be relying on the Jockey Club's claim that it could produce the money.

As the option got closer to its expiry date, 1 November, the tension mounted, but on the Friday before Davies, looking confident, arrived at Portman Square with Sue Sadler, claiming that he was ready to extend the option. To represent the Trustees, Dick Francis was on hand, Derby being in Australia. The deal that had been worked out was as follows:

> Racecourse Holdings Trust (the subsidiary of the Jockey Club) would have the rights in the 1983 Grand National for a payment now of £250,000, non-returnable. This money had been obtained from the Levy Board by way of an interest-free loan, in the normal way that interest-free loans were handed over to racecourses by the levy for development.
>
> Next, a further £250,000 was to be paid by the Jockey Club in order to obtain a new option on the course and the race, valued at £4m, to be paid by 1 May. The £250,000 was non-returnable. This money had been borrowed from Barclays, and was ready to be handed to Davies.
>
> The total to be paid to Davies, therefore, by the Club and its subsidiary, was £4½m, of which £½m was, to use the jargon, 'up front'.

While this was the deal that had been worked out, it was not, alas the deal that Davies hoped to negotiate, and the argument that followed in the Jockey Club boardroom was long and invidious.

After several hours, it was decided to sign the options, but to leave them in the hands of the lawyers until there could be another meeting later in the week, which it was hoped could be short and technical. Eventually agreement was reached between Davies and his banks and a further meeting arranged for the Friday.

Lord Vestey was at Newbury to see his horse Goldspun and told the press 'I have always been optimistic.'

In the event, the third meeting was neither short nor technical either. Davies, worried by what some of his banks were saying, tried to change the agreement yet again. It was rumoured that one of the bank representatives, angered by Davies's attitude, left the room, but was eventually persuaded to return. Henderson said 'I lost my temper' but it turned out that this had taken the form of his saying to Davies that 'We don't do business that way down here' (that is, in the City of London). The discussion went on all morning, over lunch, and through the afternoon. At one point Christopher Foster, the Jockey Club Assistant Secretary (shortly to succeed the dying Simon Weatherby) left the table to visit his wife, who worked in Buckingham Palace, taking with him all the essential papers, but returning in time to participate in the agreement which was reached about 7 p.m., nine hours after the meeting began. 'It was worth all the time it took,' said Foster.

That night the Jockey Club press office put out a statement confirming the deal, but it was worded in such a way that the following morning a large proportion of the public believed that the Grand National had in fact been 'saved' with the Jockey Club's money. This was to be a serious obstacle to fund-raising. In one sense it was true that the Jockey Club had already 'saved' the National, because Racecourse Holdings Trust, its subsidiary, had already handed over £250,000 for the right to run the 1983 race, and it could not wait to get on with the job.

A certain amount of mystery surrounds Racecourse Holdings Trust, the Jockey Club subsidiary which actually owns and operates racecourses. For example, in the *Directory of the Turf*, its only mention is under the 'Turf Officials' heading, where its Managing Director is named, but no information is given about him unless the reader looks under the cross-reference 'Owners'. No directors are given, no address or telephone number is given, nor is there a list of the racecourses owned by RHT. It might be thought that there is some deliberate mystification here.

In fact, the directors of the Trust are primarily Jockey Club members: Johnny Henderson (the Chairman), Capt. H. Miles Gosling, Chris Collins, Jocelyn Hambro and Maj. M.G. Wyatt, aided by the Managing Director, Col. Tommy Wallis and Lord Matthews (of Express Newspapers fame).

The racecourses owned and operated by the Trust are Newmarket, Cheltenham, Market Rasen, Wincanton and Haydock with leases from local authorities on Nottingham and Warwick. When the Aintree Appeal was well under way, RHT formed another subsidiary, Aintree Racecourse Ltd which had as its directors Chris Collins and Tommy Wallis of RHT plus J.P.V. Hughes, long-time clerk of the course at Aintree, who had started out his professional career at Ascot in 1954, and had been at Aintree since 1975.

From the earliest days of the Appeal, the ebullient Tommy Wallis threw himself into the organization of the 1983 race, which eventually became part of the package agreed with Davies. However, he made it clear to the fund-raisers that Aintree Racecourse Ltd must have firm control of all the promotional aspects of the race so that the income generated would be channelled to that company (whose shares were held by the Jockey Club) and would not find its way into the Appeal. So anxious was he to make the point, that after a meeting when clerk of the course John Hughes threatened to resign if he did not retain full authority over the negotiations of TV rights, the fund-raisers were obliged to write Wallis a letter agreeing that RHT had control over all such matters.

This led to no little misunderstanding. The fund-raisers had thought that they would be able to offer prospective donors the opportunity to advertise on jumps, and even to rename such famous locations as Becher's for the benefit of advertisers. RHT held various meetings at which they encouraged the fund-raisers to pursue this concept. The advantage was that business and industry, instead of giving to the Appeal, would be able to divert funds from their advertising budgets, with considerable tax as well as promotional advantages.

It will be recalled that David Montagu and Johnny Henderson, meeting at the Turf Club, had spent much time speculating on the money that a company like Coca Cola would pay for half a dozen fences. All this was to come to nothing. Early in November, once the deal with Davies had been signed, RHT appeared for a meeting with the fund-raisers and asserted, without explanation, that no fences would be available to the Appeal, although a small number of banners would be offered, together with some modest promotional opportunities elsewhere. In the early heady days of the campaign, sums such as £500,000 had been talked about as income from advertising – and in five minutes it disappeared after a speech by John Hughes. The fund-raisers felt the disappointment keenly, but Wallis and Hughes, who had to find £250,000 to pay Davies for the rent of the course, were pleased that this income at least was going where it should belong.

Another curious volte face on the part of RHT concerned its attitude to the 'recreational area' on the racecourse, the 100 acres defined as charitable in the agreement reached with the Charity Commissioners. In the early days of the Merseyside County Council's involvement with the negotiations, Chris Collins, representing Aintree Racecourse Ltd, had gone to great pains to put the company on good terms with the Council in the expectation that they would play a considerable part in drawing up plans for the recreational area. At the time of the public launch he said, 'we would want to make a wholesale contribution to life on Merseyside'. He and representatives of the Council had walked round the course looking at the various facilities and discussing what might be done. The assumption was that Aintree Racecourse Ltd would involve itself not only in the organization of the race, but also in the activities to be developed on the racecourse, with the help of the Council, on a year-round basis.

Collins mentioned various possibilities such as sports facilities for the handicapped, tennis courts, squash and athletics.

The fund-raisers expressed the view at this point that the charitable area – that is, the 100 acres – would have to be regarded as separate from the remainder of the course, and money donated to it would have to be defined as having a separate purpose from that given to the Appeal.

Again, Tommy Wallis took a new direction, claiming that he had not understood this, and that in the circumstances Aintree Racecourse Ltd would have nothing whatever to do with the

100-acre area, with the associated year-round recreational facilities, or with anything other than the running of the three-day event culminating in the National. Despite this, Chris Collins was to talk later of building new grandstands as part of a redevelopment scheme to make Aintree 'the great new sports hall of the North'.

Having established these points of principle, Wallis set about the crux of his task – getting the 1983 race organized on a commercial basis. Since about June 1982, Aintree Racecourse Ltd had been financially responsible for the staff on the ground at Aintree – about a dozen people formerly employed by Davies. Their knowledge of the course, the grandstand and the rest of the infrastructure was vital to the satisfactory condition of the grounds. In the dark and difficult days before the deal with Davies was clinched, Chris Collins made several visits to Liverpool to speak to the staff and to reassure them, as best he could, about the future.

The other commercial aspects of the race fell into the hands of Hughes, clerk of the course, who had for many years negotiated the TV rights, and the sponsorship by Rupert Murdoch's newspaper interests. These proved complex and difficult but Hughes was confident that he would, once again, succeed in getting an income from these two sources which would match the £250,000 already paid to Davies. By January, negotiations were still moving slowly. Hughes had a £12,000 purse from Kaltenberg Pils Lager, the Holiday Inn hotel at Liverpool had offered a new £6,000 race as well as one of £5,000, and John Haig Whisky offered £5,000.

In the old days, the Adelphi Hotel had been synonymous with the race, but now it was the Holiday Inn, just down the road from the course. The manager, explaining his increased involvement in the racing, said: 'It does a tremendous amount for both the Liverpool community and the hotel trade, so we think that it is important that those who benefit from the meeting should also contribute. That is why we have decided to increase our support this year and to sponsor a second race.

'Furthermore, the hotel will be making a donation to the "Appeal Fund" which has been set up to save Aintree and with it the National. This sum will be made up from both donations made by Holiday Inn guests and a donation from the hotel for every room sold during the meeting. The target figure will be £2,000.'

As regards the promotion and administration of the race itself, Wallis put this in the hands of an outside commercial organization, which had previously worked with Ladbrokes, during the period after they had been responsible for the race, under their arrangement with Davies.

Thus, Wallis and his two associates on the board of the newly-formed Aintree Racecourse Ltd, had succeeded in setting up an organization to mount perhaps the world's most popular race, consisting of less than a dozen or so groundsmen at Aintree, a firm of outside consultants, and a back-up team of secretarial and accountancy services at the Portman Square offices of the Jockey Club. Rarely can so much have been in the hands of so few.

At the public launch, Chris Collins said, 'We are taking on a viable business. It is not necessary to consider extra days' racing. Staging the world's greatest steeplechase is in itself a viable business.'

Collins added that the current life expectancy of the grandstands was another two years, and he stressed they would be quite safe even with a capacity crowd of 55,000. The plan then was eventually either to demolish the stands and replace them with a platform, on which he could erect temporary seating, or else build new stands.

John Fennell of Merseyside County Council said at the public launch, 'We would like to see the course used throughout the year, with the land developed for the use of Merseyside.' Rejecting accusations that Merseyside had done nothing to date to salvage the National, Mr Fennell said there was an all-party commitment to saving the race, and Lord Vestey talked of the 'heartwarming feeling' the MCC had for the race.

It remained to be seen if Merseyside would put its money where its mouth was.

15: The Appeal to the Public

The professional fund-raisers had circulated a document describing the preconditions to be met before public fund-raising could begin. This asserted that before donations could be realistically sought from sources outside those immediately involved in the Grand National, and outside the country, early conditional gifts must be provided from the four sectors closest to the Appeal: (1) the Jockey Club; (2) leading owners, trainers and jockeys; (3) bookmakers and (4) Liverpool. Privately the fund-raisers believed that until the Jockey Club made its own donation, even the other three 'insiders' would lag behind, and furthermore that until Vestey made his donation, the rest of the Jockey Club would prevaricate.

So until the Jockey Club achieved its half-million target, the owners, trainers and jockeys their £1m, the bookmakers their £1m and Liverpool its £350,000, there should be no question of going to the public, or to the overseas groups who, it was hoped, would bring in £750,000.

An elaborate plan was drawn up to tackle the Jockey Club membership reversing the principle, as the fund-raisers put it 'that if the trumpet gives an uncertain sound who shall follow?' Initially, some four top Stewards should donate, and they would then each press two others for a donation of similar significance (that is to say, another large sum of the order of £25,000–£50,000 each). Names were listed, so that it was clear who should be asked and by whom. The final series of contacts would result in about half the members of the Club being approached in a very direct way, the assumption being that the other half could not or would not give substantially if at all. A table was drawn up to show how the £½m would be broken down between this half of the membership, starting with a large gift of £50,000 and smaller sums of £5,000. It will be recalled that some dozen members had each contributed £5,000 to the running of the office, and they might wish to convert this to a donation to the Appeal. Finally, it was thought some members would rather make a simple pledge now, and donate cash later.

Time and again, the fund-raisers reiterated that there should be no public appeal until after what they described as stage 1, when the interested parties had been tapped. At that stage they estimated that a public broad-based appeal should have a target of £½m. Alas, all these plans were to be drastically redrawn.

The first blow came from the bookmakers. The betting industry was going through a somewhat difficult time, but the public might be forgiven for thinking that, like farmers, book-makers were always going through a difficult time. The fund-raisers had hoped to have a private meeting with Ladbrokes to discuss tactics, but to their chagrin, the somewhat impulsive Col. Tommy Wallace arranged for the bookies to invite the Appeal to lunch with them instead.

In the morning of 7 September the Bookmakers' Committee representing the big four (Ladbrokes, William Hill, Coral and Mecca) and representatives of the smaller bookmakers met in the Connaught Rooms and told Tristram Ricketts of the Levy Board that their businesses were in such dire straits that the usual contribution from profits to the Levy would not, this year, be forthcoming. They put the decline in income down to the recession. More betting shops had closed down in the first half of 1982 than in the whole of 1981. Bookies were almost the only members of the community who could not raise their prices – you could not ask a punter accustomed to place a £1 bet to make it £1.20. The Levy Board listened but did not cry.

At lunch-time they filed into the room next door and plied themselves with drink awaiting the arrival of Lord Vestey, Col. Tommy Wallace and the fund-raisers. As they sat down to their smoked salmon, Sam Vestey quickly sketched in the current state of the Appeal. After their steak, the bookmakers followed the same line they had presented to the Levy Board that morning – they were broke. Furthermore they had little use for the Grand National which brought in no income. Sam Vestey put forward the view that it encouraged an interest in racing, and hence in betting.

Not so said the bookies. For example, the Prince of Wales (Edward VIII) had opened an account with William Hill in the 1930s, but had only ever bet on the National, and this was typical. The National only brought in small bets (despite the fact that it was the world's most heavily backed race, one-third more money being placed on it than on the Derby). Furthermore said the bookies, £4m or £3m was far too much money for the racecourse – £800,000 was nearer the mark. Finally the representative of Ladbrokes who had run the race for several years said he must recommend to his board a lack of interest in the race and the Appeal until a more realistic purchase price was reached. It would not matter in the least if the race disappeared for two years. His colleagues shouted assent over their brandies and port.

Sam Vestey stood up to thank his hosts for lunch. 'As a butcher,' he said, 'I am delighted that despite your dire straits you can still manage to serve a good steak.'

The bookmakers' annual results may not support their assertion that profits were substantially down, partly because they have other interests than betting shops and do not extract their results on their own. But both Ladbrokes and William Hill, with 2,000 shops between them, made noises about their sad state. All in all, the prospect of the Appeal realizing a £1m donation from the bookies looked slender indeed.

The campaign to tackle the owners and trainers also got off to a slow start. There had been a lunch in the Cavalry and Guards' Club in Piccadilly attended by a wide range of owners. The *Daily Express* heard about it and got in a dig that at last the listless Jockey Club was getting up steam, although what came out of the lunch was not money, or even promises of cash, but only the formation of an owners' group under Nick Embiricos. He developed an elaborate and expensive system of letters to individual owners, 16,000 of them, seeking donations, and to add authenticity to the Appeal Bob Champion promised that he would sign a significant proportion of the letters and had completed a total of 1,000 by the end of January 1983. Regrettably, by the end of January, very little money had come in from owners as a group.

But despite the fact that not one of the fund-raisers' targets had been met, the Jockey Club felt it could delay no longer in going public. It had promised to do so in the New Year, and the end of January just about qualified for that description. So at a press conference on 28 January, Sam Vestey officially launched the Appeal and gave a broad-brush picture of what had been achieved. The veracity of the figures was later questioned.

£1m already raised (it had been expected to have £3½m before going public) of which £300,000 was from the Jockey Club (the target had been £500,000).
£1.5m expected from UK, USA, Ireland and Australia.
£1m to £1.5m expected from general public (originally £½m).

This barely added up to £4m, and in fact more than that total was needed to cover Davies's bill and the administrative expenses of the Appeal. As for the other anticipated donations expected before the public launch, 'discussions are in progress with the bookies' said Lord Vestey. 'The Merseyside County Council, the various borough councils involved and most prominent businessmen in the area could not be more concerned and could not have been more helpful. But as everyone knows Liverpool has been badly hit by the recession and many local charities are finding it difficult to raise funds.' So said Lord Derby – in other words, no money is to be expected from Liverpool. Finally, £25,000 from two trust funds, out of the target of £500,000.

The fund-raisers had therefore made a significant miscalculation in believing that £3½m could be in sight before going to the public for the balance of £½m; the public target was now as high as £1½m and there was only, as Sam Vestey put it, ninety-four days to bring it in. That averaged out to £15,000 a day including Sundays.

How could it be done? Some newspapers seemed to be in no doubt that it could. 'Money looks no obstacle' was the headline in *The Times*. 'National Appeal launched on an optimistic note', said the *Telegraph*. *Horse and Hound*, more cautious, said 'the future of the Grand National is in no way assured'. With only £1m in the fund and £1½m anticipated from the public, this left at least another £1½m from other vested interests, which averaged out at a further £15,000 a day, making £30,000 a day in all if £4m was to be reached by 1 May. This should be contrasted with the £4,000 a day or less which had been the average receipts since the fund-raisers moved into the Jockey Club. Was the new target achievable?

Among the public attractions offered at the launch were:

Special efforts to raise funds would be made at the Cheltenham meeting. (These did not materialize.)

There would be five extra point-to-point meetings to raise funds (although it would be remarkable if each raised more than £5,000 for the Appeal).

On 22 March, Whitbreads would put the Porter and Tun room at their brewery at the disposal of the Appeal, with a free dinner for 400 guests at which the journalist Peter O'Sullevan would auction gifts for the Appeal.

There would be special Grand National days at racecourses, attended by Red Rum. Manager Peter Rougier had offered the heroic horse to any organization which would pay the expenses of horse and groom.

At Ascot there would be a party in April to which all living owners, trainers and jockeys of past Grand National winners would be invited.

A company called Aircall promoted a credit card system for making payments by telephone.

A Grand National ball was to be held in the Rainbow Suite, Kensington on 7 April.

John Francome, Lord Oaksey, Brough Scott, Oliver Sherwood and three others would take part in the London marathon.

A memorial fund was opened for Roger Ward, a recent Master of the Worcestershire Hunt, an example par excellence, said *Horse and Hound*, of the 'sporting English gentleman' and every penny would go to the Aintree Appeal.

Two weeks later, Lord Vestey said that in the first week following the Appeal, the public had given £87,000. On this basis it would take seventeen weeks to collect £1½m and there was only twelve weeks to go. Vestey ignored these statistical realities and instead recounted how out of 800 letters he had received, only ten were against the race. Among the most curious of these letters was one from the Duke of Beaufort's stables, where a stable lad who had refrained from biting his fingernails for a week, had been 'sponsored' to the tune of several pounds by his colleagues.

One section of the public that might be expected to have a particular interest in the Grand National was the citizenry of Liverpool. How much did they care about the racecourse and the race? For a TV programme on the city, the researchers asked thirty Liverpudlians if they would mind if the National disappeared. Not one of them expressed any real regret. This may have been due to the fact that the Aintree meeting was a one-day (or strictly three-day) event, and the locals had long ago given up hope of having an all-the-year round entertainment centre on their doorstep, despite the efforts made by Mirabel Topham with her motor-racing and Ladbrokes' schemes for flat racing and parachute jumping. All such enterprises seemed doomed to failure.

As long ago as 1909 there had been demonstrations of flying on the racecourse, Sir William Hartley, the jam manufacturer, having offered £1,000 for the first flight from Aintree to Manchester in which Col. Cody took part.

The clerk of the course, John Hughes, who had seen the books for a good many Aintree events, gave it as his opinion that no race there, except the Grand National, had ever made a profit. So if you couldn't make money on the horseracing – except the National – and you couldn't make money on the non-racing activities, what did the local citizens want to do with Aintree?

One of the most prominent of the locals is Sir John Moore, who made his fortune by running, rather than winning, football pools. When the Appeal to save Aintree was announced, he said he was very doubtful if the Jockey Club would raise the money. 'You only have to look at the place to see what needs doing,' he said. 'They will have to find another £4m or £5m to do the place up. I certainly wish them every success but I would have to consider carefully before I would add my own support.' Another football pools promoter who was not very forthcoming about his support was Robert Sangster, who had become a member of the Jockey Club as a protégé, according to rumours in Portman Square, of Lord Leverhulme.

The proposal put forward with the greatest energy was to develop 'environmental' activities while retaining the National as a one-day or three-day event. It will be recalled that this was what the charitable element of the Aintree Appeal was designed to fund. The immediately obvious drawback to Aintree as 'environmental' was that it was so scruffy and could never be a beauty spot. Clement Freud, the well-known *bon viveur* and owner, called it 'a dilapidated and run-down racecourse'.

Despite this, the Merseyside County Council constantly made growling noises about a compulsory purchase order (it may be doubted how serious this really was) coupled with the desirability of a sports complex of some kind. Mr John Fernell, a member of the Council, said that some sixty possible activities, including watersports, had been suggested for Aintree but that nothing could be planned until the ownership changed.

There appeared to be a dichotomy between the racing experts and those who wished to 'develop'. Collins of RHT claimed that the three-day National event meeting was financially viable and no more fixtures were required – indeed it was not practical to hold any. At the same time, he said that he was planning talks with the MCC over the possibility of building a recreational scheme which would provide leisure facilities for the people of Liverpool, and part of which could be used as a grandstand. It might well be asked, if Aintree was viable on a three-day basis, empty for the remaining 349 days, then why hold, or plan to hold, talks with MCC about recreational facilities?

One factor in the equation was that Merseyside County Council had indicated that while no ratepayers' money would be available to develop Aintree, there might well be public money which could be applied to its environmental improvement. Walking round the course with Chris Collins, an MCC official explained that there were central government-approved funds for demolishing decrepit buildings, or for converting or constructing buildings for the disabled or the young. Collins was reluctant to give up the prospect of a development of this kind, despite the fact that RHT's managing director Tommy Wallis had no interest in it, nor did the clerk of the course, Hughes.

So right through the period of the Aintree Appeal, from mid-1982 onwards, enthusiastic noises continued to be heard about some 'development' at Aintree for the good of the citizens of Liverpool.

One cannot escape the suspicion that the Merseyside County Council were engaged in a political game, blowing hot about support for the environmental centre, and blowing cool when it came to any commitment, in case the Jockey Club's public appeal ended in failure. Evidence for this view is the leaflet which they handed out to racegoers at the 1983 National. MCC said 'Conditions for both the owner and the punter have deteriorated. The grandstands are near the ends of their lives. The racing calendar is reduced to a single three-day meeting. Had it not been for the Grand National the course should have closed long ago. These 260 acres of land should not lie largely unused for most of the year for the sake of twenty minutes' glory . . . Merseyside County Council working with the Jockey Club are hoping to stimulate development at Aintree . . . Merseyside County Council believes that other activities as well as horse-racing should be introduced for the benefit of the people of Merseyside and far beyond.'

The Council went on to list the ideas that had been put forward for Aintree over the years. Redeveloping the grandstands to incorporate indoor sports halls and restaurants, an hotel and casino, an indoor athletics or tennis stadium, the reintroduction of motor-racing and cycling, a riding school or equestrian centre, a golf course, a park and a boating marina . . . The County Council 'cannot promise that any particular scheme can be carried out . . . but it would appreciate your views'. It therefore distributed several thousand leaflets asking the punters to give their views. The questions asked were 'As a racegoer, what facilities would you like to see provided at Aintree?' and 'If it is possible to provide other facilities, what would you suggest?' In passing, it would be interesting to know what the Charity Commissioners would think about a development on the 'charity' land, a main feature of which might be a casino.

Reading the leaflet, it was impossible not to avoid the view that we were going round in circles.

Perhaps the people of Liverpool did not, in truth, feel all that strongly about Aintree, which had originally been a village outside, and was not incorporated in Liverpool until 1909. They had many more pressing priorities. The cathedral was falling down (it had only been built in 1967) and its railway station was under attack – a Euro MP said he would not keep pigs in the loo. No, the professional fund-raisers' aim to get £350,000 out of Liverpool seemed undoubtedly optimistic.

16: The Public and the Jockey Club

At a time when the Jockey Club was in the process of deciding, in desperation, that it would need three times as much money from the public as it originally envisaged, it is interesting to ask what the public in general thought about the Club. The answer is that it probably thought very little, in the sense that it knew very little. This was to change as soon as that mighty medium TV began to take a hand. The journalist Ivor Herbert, who had made the American appeal film for the Jockey Club, at the Levy Board's expense, had for some while been negotiating with Simon Weatherby to make a film about the Club. It would be made by Herbert's friends at Yorkshire TV who had made the Appeal film and Herbert agreed it would meet the general wishes of the Club.

The critics' opinion of the film, which was shown nationally on ITV, can probably be taken to approximate to the public's. Headlines like 'Slanted TV view did not alter the face of autocracy' (*Sporting Chronicle*) and 'Suspicion remains after TV programme' (the *Racehorse*) indicated that the experts were not taken in: Nancy Banks-Smith of the *Guardian*, not an expert, noted that 'The Jockey Club is so-called because it is not a club for jockeys. Half the members have handles to their names and the other half, I would hazard, have hyphens. Nevertheless, feeling like the rest of us, insufficiently appreciated, the Jockey Club opened its doors, or rather its tradesman's entrance, to

TV.' She refers to the paintings and decorations at Newmarket
. . . 'I said to Lester Piggott we might end up having his skin in a
case. Ha. Ha,' said Lord Howard de Walden, a genial former
Senior Steward. The *Mail* called this a 24-carat chump's remark.

Another critic said that 'incredibly there is not a single word
about the Jockey Club's future from the present Senior Steward
Lord Manton. It is as though a documentary on the Tory party
interviewed Ted Heath and Harold Macmillan, recalled the
historical roles of Disraeli and Churchill and yet failed to talk to
Margaret Thatcher.'

Another criticism was 'why are inquiries still secret?' 'The
composition of the Jockey Club', and 'its threat to decimate the
fixture list if more levy was not squeezed from bookmakers and
pirates', were never mentioned. 'Nor is the financial story behind
the purchase and running of the Jockey Club racecourses by
Racecourse Holdings Trust. Or the alleged "cosmetic" nature of
the Horseracing Advisory Council.' These comments by John
McCririck are from the informed public rather than the public in
general.

But what took up most of the film, and made most impression,
was that jockeys' inquiries were shown with full documentary
fervour. 'The jockeys like serfs in medieval times, are still
addressed curtly as "Carson" or "Hide" without the courtesy of
Mister, and they deferentially refer to their "betters" as "Sir".
This is just a quaint anachronism.' Nancy Banks-Smith said 'the
stewards had a headmasterish air and Jockey Club justice does
somehow suggest Keate of Eton'. 'It is horrible, an embarrassing
anchronism which, since the Jockey Club allowed it to be filmed,
shows how out of touch it is.'

According to the critics, the right to change factual material
was written into the Club's contract with Yorkshire. Be that as it
may the result was seen as opting 'for the easy way out by doing a
Madison Avenue-style PR job which will delight the image-
conscious Portman Square'. 'The unspoken belief in a divine
right to rule was there for all to see.' 'As far as the Club was
concerned, this programme was obviously intended to be an
exercise in public relations, and although occasional reference to
inadequacy in high places was permitted, it was always in
connection with the past. This may have been the price Yorkshire
TV had to pay for admission; this and the answers to any really

relevant questions about the Club's right and suitability to continue to govern.' The *Daily Mail* said 'All that was lacking was the occasional "What Ho" to anchor it firmly in the pages of a P.G. Wodehouse comedy.' The *Mail* added this was 'a self-perpetuating dynasty with absolute power over British racing'.

The Club remains the 'most élitist and undemocratic ruling body in sport, in spite of its reliance on public money'. To conclude the press reports: 'Horseracing may be the sport of Kings, but it is undoubtedly supported by the nation's cabbages.'

A token radical was included in the film, in the form of Lord Wigg, who commented that if the Jockey Club doesn't change, it will end up 'like the dinosaur – stuffed'. The reception given to the programme was indeed so severe that Lord Wigg was emboldened to write to *The Times* saying that the savage criticism following the televison programme caused him to write in the Club's defence, but he then proceeded to write a reasoned but low-key attack on it. No one wrote to *The Times* in its defence. Indeed, in the Club, Wigg's letter was ignored. Simon Weatherby's reaction was typical: he said that 'he had had to put up with all that same nonsense from Wigg during his time at the Levy Board, and he wasn't going to pay any attention to it now in the newspapers'.

Those who are very set in their ways do not find it possible to see themselves as others see them, and this was the Jockey Club's reaction to the Stewards' inquiry on TV. There was nothing wrong with it, they said, because this was how they were. But when, three months later, TV struck again, they realized that the picture drawn of them was critical, and reacted accordingly. The subject this time was not the Jockey Club as such, but a charity operating within its aegis, the Stable Lads' Welfare Trust. Stable lads are said by some to be unprivileged members of society, earning as little as £5 for a sixty-hour week in some cases, and being without benefit of a union. There are some 25,000 grooms and the upper echelons earn £25, it is said, for a sixty-hour week.

One might conclude, said *The Times*, that stable lads have nothing to fear in the way of welfare, recreation, poverty or sickness, all of which the Trust is there to attend to but 'such a conclusion appears to be wrong'. The TV programme dealt with a usual annual shindig in a Park Lane hotel held allegedly to raise funds for the Trust, and which raised £65,578 out of a total annual income of £120,293. It was reported, said *The Times*, that the Trust's administrative expenses for that year were £34,530; that there was £251,819 held in cash at the bank; and that the Trust's total assets were £431,287. The TV programme reported that £53,529 had been spent on recreational facilities but only £569 on relief.

The Chairman of the Trust, Sir James D'Avigor-Goldsmith (Harrow, the Jockey Club and sometimes Levy Board representative), wrote to the newspaper at once to complain about the programme. He accused the producer of failing to honour an agreement not to spell out the precise detail of expenses, although the producer in reply pointed out that it was expenditure which was in question. The BBC had had to go to the Trust for the figures because 'as a registered charity the Trust's accounts should be a matter for public record but [there had been] failure to lodge any accounts with the Charity Commissioners since 1976'. When the accounts for 1981 arrived, said the BBC producer, 'there appeared to be a remarkable discrepancy between the Trust's stated aims and the use to which the money was put'. Sir James thought the programme showed 'lack of taste in the scenes of intoxication' at the party, and *The Times* reviewer said that the 'racing and sporting guests were at their best to answer questions, being emboldened by food and drink and the heady warmth of camaraderie into behaving before the camera in a way they may subsequently reflect on as unwise'.

Sir James explained that he had decided, 'needless to say', to decline the BBC's offer to appear on the programme.

All this left a nasty taste in the mouth and the scapegoat, in the Club's views, was the BBC. It was put about that professional actors had been used to pose as guests to the dinner. True, this was not a programme about the Jockey Club as such, but the guests were from the upper echelons of racing, and the public, subject to all this TV documentary interest, could be excused for thinking that those in charge of the Turf were not living the life which 'the other half lived'. The press continued, in the main, to be critical of the Club's handling of the Appeal, especially so some of the sporting columnists.

17: The Outcome

How he must regret it, Lord Howard de Walden, that is, who when Senior Steward, declared that as far as the Jockey Club was concerned, power was the name of the game. This is power of a particular sort, too, because it is power over a pastime that rich men enjoy almost above all others. And not only the rich members, but those they employ, the Club's permanent staff whose duty it is to leave their offices several days a week and go off to racecourses, festooned with badges, both to administer and to enjoy racing. So the power not only to control the whole paraphernalia but also to enjoy it as well is within their grasp, not like a Member of Parliament for an elected period, but, by and large, for ever. No self-respecting member of the Jockey Club would ever have heard of the late Kenneth Tynan, but they would agree with him when he said, 'All power is delightful and absolute power is absolutely delightful.' What the Jockey Club has is not just power, but absolute power. So it is fair to discuss in what mode that absolute power resides and how it is exercised.

The Times put it like this: 'The Jockey Club's functions and responsibilities extend to every aspect of racing. It draws up, administers and enforces the rules of racing; it is the disciplinary body for breaches of the rules; it is the licensing body for jockeys and trainers [and racecourses] and has the power to take away their livelihood if they offend against the rules. It has its own investigation squad, provides security services for racecourses, and camera patrols and photofinish equipment for the races themselves. It controls the testing of horses for drugs. The stewards – unpaid – are at every race meeting to ensure that the rules are complied with and to settle disputes. It lays down the weight and financial conditions at races. One of its most important functions is to determine the fixture list. No race can be run without the Jockey Club's approval [so] the result is that the Levy Board has, in effect, to bribe racecourses to hold meetings before a handful of spectators on a wet Thursday in February. The day to day administration of racing is carried out by Weatherby's, a family firm, under contract to the Jockey Club. The runners and riders for every race, the weights, the draw, the handicapping system, even the allocation of owners' colours, are all handled through their offices [and even the horses' names, they might have said]. The accounts are there too. The entry fees come in, and the prize money goes out to the fortunate. . . All this – the entire administration of racing – operates on a budget which *this year* [not 1983] will be about £3 million. The Jockey Club's income comes mainly from fees received from racecourses for various services rendered, from entry fees, and from charges for licences, permits and registrations. The bulk of the expenditure goes to pay Weatherby's and for the salaries of racecourse personnel.'

This then is where the absolute power resides. Right through racing, from top to bottom, 'the entire administration of racing' is in the hands of a body of self-elected men, and their paid staff and contractors, Weatherby's, who are an unlimited company and publish no accounts or give any account of themselves. Good enough, but, by your works shall ye be known, and *The Times* says, 'It is highly efficient and not at all old-fashioned in outlook.' It also says, 'To criticize the Jockey Club for being an élitist, self-perpetuating body drawn largely from a particular social class is to miss the point. The question should be: how well does it run racing? The answer to that is that its administration is efficient, relatively cheap, because so many of its services are provided by volunteers, and utterly honest.'

So *The Times* is saying what many of its defenders would claim it is the fair thing to say, that its operations may not be open to the light of day (for example its inquiries into racing are held *in camera*) but it works. And since it works, then leave it alone, and do not complain about what are largely academic matters of 'fairness'. Indeed *The Times* goes one further and seems to imply that even if one wanted to change the system one couldn't because 'for one thing the Jockey Club and its satellites have the monopoly of knowledge and experience of running racing' so there is nothing to be done about it.

It is true that very rarely does the Jockey Club make a move in the direction of what the Americans call disclosure. In 1970, the Club applied to the Privy Council for a Royal Charter, which would save it from having to become a private limited company, by acquiring all the advantages of incorporation with none of the disadvantages – no accounts to be published, no directors named and so on. Bodies that are both posh and old are invariably granted this Charter if they ask for it. The Club could then face the 1970s knowing that from a legal point of view they had protection of a kind, and the benefits of continued secrecy. Weatherby's too, who were contracted by the Club to administer their policies, took steps to protect themselves by registering as an unlimited company, describing the members of the family, in the process, as 'publishers', which was hardly frank.

Some critics claim that the Jockey Club misuses its monopolistic and absolute power in certain respects. Lord Wigg is one. He claims that the Jockey Club has maintained positions which have enabled it to exercise decisive power without regard to the economic consequences. The Jockey Club, he says, is still over-represented on the Levy Board, and the Board's policy in recent years has been to accept domination of the Jockey Club and to spend the levy on excessive grants for prize money and interest-free loans to Jockey Club courses. This was not, Lord Wigg argues, the intention of Parliament when it passed the bill setting up the Levy Board, and the Home Secretary now, who should have been carrying out these intentions, has too often been forced into a position in which his reason points in one direction and Jockey Club pressures have pointed in another. Levy Board money also goes to support the breeding of horses, the livestock business, in which members of the Jockey Club have many a vested interest.

As critic of the Jockey Club system, Lord Wigg complains that the Levy was not intended to subsidize racing, but that the horseracing industry is today wholly dependent upon subsidy.

He quotes the Report of the Royal Commission on Gambling: 'The industry is today hopelessly addicted to subsidy – withdrawal would mean collapse.'

Another harsh critic is Phil Bull, one-time chairman of the Horserace Advisory Council, allegedly an advisory body to the Levy Board, but, few would disagree, a toothless one. His point is that racing is part of the entertainments industry. He says that all taxpayers, including punters, are called upon to foot the bill for theatre, opera, ballet, art and music; but only punters are called upon to foot the bill for horseracing, which is subsidized not by direct grants from the Treasury but by punters' money, through the levy on betting. And the power struggle today, he says, is about who gets his hands on the punters' money and who decides how it is to be spent. The entertainment is provided in the form of 7 per cent on the racecourse, and 93 per cent on television, but Bull claims that the entertainment lies essentially in the betting. So the punter is the paying customer for racing entertainment, and all the entertainers, bar the horse, are after his money. Thus, concludes Bull, in a democratic society it might be supposed that an entertainment industry like this, heavily subsidized at the punters' expense, should at least be controlled and administered by a body answerable to the people involved in the industry. But it is run by an undemocratic and élite private club which is answerable to no one, and does not even publish its accounts. It makes the rules. True, the Levy Board holds the purse strings, but the Levy Board is now firmly in the embrace of the Jockey Club.

In support of his contention, Phil Bull refers to the Blue Report, by a Committee of Inquiry composed of the three Home Office-appointed members of the Levy Board and three members of the Jockey Club. It was unveiled by Lord Plummer in April 1980. The Report itself contained no evidence and was prepared without prior consultation with any racing interests. It was said to have been written by a famous Jockey Club member, Lord Weinstock, with two senior Club members, Maj. Michael Wyatt and Mr Louis Freedman at his elbow. All three are owner-breeders with either strings of horses in training or substantial breeding interests, and the Report was heavily loaded in that direction. In fact it was little more than a statement of how the wealthier owner-breeders would like to see the levy distributed to their own better advantage, concludes Phil Bull, himself an owner-breeder. Roughly speaking it proposed a heavy transfer of prize money support from the minor Flat racecourses which needed it most, to the major establishment racecourses which needed it least. Mr Bull goes on to describe how the capital for the major fashionable National Hunt racecourses would be handed out and denied to the lesser courses. He describes this as a scheme to hand out more punters' money to wealthy owner-breeders and less to the little owners of modest horses, with unfortunate economic consequences for the latter.

This is described as a typical élitist Jockey Club exercise which Lord Plummer railroaded through, and was implemented with minor modifications in 1981 and still remains, Mr Bull presumes, Levy Board policy. Because the Jockey Club is so strongly represented on the Levy Board, year after year, its demand for more prize money has been met, to be distributed in accordance with its policies, and the Board year after year satisfies its insatiable appetite. There is no sign of protection for the betting public because the Levy Board has swallowed Jockey Club policies hook, line and sinker.

The Jockey Club's three nominees on the Levy Board are there to represent not only Jockey Club interests, but also those of the racing industry as a whole, and in order to provide this latter function, the Club put one of its seats at the disposal of the Horserace Advisory Council. The chairman of the Board and two other members are nominated by the Secretary of State to protect the public interest. These two *ex-officio* members are the chairman of the Bookmakers' Committee and the chairman of the Tote, and, as neither is a beneficiary from Levy Board funds, they are presumed to be impartial. According to Phil Bull, this Levy Board structure weights matters in practice in favour of Jockey Club policies.

It seems fair to ask for more evidence to support the charge that there is a problem of principle here. After all, in looking after its own interests, the Club provides an entertainment industry for the punters, and, even if it somehow doesn't seem the best way of going about it, the Club's operations amount in the words of *The Times*, to an administration which is efficient, relatively cheap and utterly honest.

By trying to extend their control of racing to the Grand

National as well, criticism has been levelled at the Club, as we have seen, on the grounds that it is composed of rich men who could well afford to buy Aintree by putting their hands in their own pockets. Of course, a rich Club member can all too easily be criticized for not making a large contribution to the Aintree Appeal. But surely others, notably the bookmakers, who have a very direct interest in the outcome of the Aintree Appeal, are the much more to be blamed for not digging into their wallets, indeed hardly getting their fingers within reach of the relevant pocket. *Horse and Hound* said, 'it would be prudent of the bookmakers to pay a larger sum of the capital needed' and even after the four leading bookmakers paid £25,000 each to the Appeal, *The Times* attacked them for not having done enough, bearing in mind that fourteen million fairly regular punters stake £30m on the race, and that the bookmaking industry took over two and a half *billion* pounds in bets last year in total.

The moment of truth came on 1 May 1983 when the Jockey Club added up the donations received, deducted the considerable expenses involved in the Appeal, and found that the total plus the pledges (that is, promises to donate if the Appeal succeeded) fell short of the total required by about £2m.

The highlights of the Appeal in its final stages illustrated that those closest to the race were doing something, but it was too little if not too late. The fund-raisers had hustled out a leaflet which claimed that the Aintree Appeal would be aided by an exclusive Grand National collection of prestigious items, compiled by the Campaign Committee. This comprised two Husky waistcoats, a sweat-shirt, a V-necked jumper, a kid's T-shirt, a tie, a scarf and so on. Slightly more prestigious, to use their phrase, was a bone china plate at £27.50, featuring steeplechasing highlights and a decanter and glasses at £250. There was a limited edition of a map of the course dating back to 1925 at £44.95 and, finally, a tea towel in 100 per cent Irish cotton at £1.75 plus postage, packing and insurance at £0.75, that is £2.50 in all. The retail sale of these items organized by another group of professionals, the Great British T-Shirt Company, was very slow, and money was actually lost at most of the smaller race meetings, and a visit to the Scottish Grand National was cancelled, as it would never have paid. Only a couple of thousand tea towels were printed, and the big items like the decanters sold in tiny numbers. The organizers nevertheless thought they might cover the £10,000 they had promised the Club, but not much more. Other more plebeian ways of collecting money were employed such as sending Red Rum to Haydock Park and taking round collecting tins, but the results were not good and the cash collected was minimal. Even at the popular Cheltenham meeting, there was no collection for the Appeal; the professional fund-raisers claimed, 'We have hit people at the racecourse right, left and centre and we do not want to be a nuisance. We found it more valuable just to talk to people and to explain that without their money there might be no Grand National after this year.' Most serious of all there were no collecting tins to be seen at the 1983 National race itself, not at the entrance gate, nor at the stands, although money was collected for the unemployed of Liverpool. Tea towels etc. were sold on the course and Lord Vestey declared the results of a raffle, but only £4,500 was said to have been raised from the public that day, 9 April, with less than three weeks to go before the option expired.

It will be recalled that as long ago as the 1982 National, the press were critical that the Jockey Club had missed its opportunity to start the Appeal with official donation boxes at Aintree where there had been a crowd of 65,000. The excuse then given by the prominent member of Racecourse Holdings Trust was that 'it was felt that with time to go home and reflect on the epic they had witnessed, racegoers would be inclined to give more generously'. A journalist commented, 'I still find it difficult [a year later] to believe that anyone could think that way.' So once again, the press were critical of the lack of effort in 1983.

Donations from the 16,000 owners were well below expectations; despite all the grandeur of being an owner, when Nick Embiricos wrote asking for a donation, they gave on average (according to *The Times*) a mere £4 each. The City, too, had been a disappointment and the auction laid on by Whitbreads at their Tun Room had raised £35,000. The ball in Kensington raised considerably less, and was not one of the highlights of the social season, with Lord Derby committing a solecism by proposing the Loyal Toast (that is, allowing the diners to smoke) immediately after the starter had been served and before some guests were seated.

So all this had been in terms of public support, or in hard cash from the racing fraternity, disappointing. The Jockey Club itself claimed to have £½m from members and RHT Ltd, and The Times said Sam Vestey had already contributed 'more than handsomely himself'. The Americans, who had aimed at 1 million dollars, only brought in half that. Great efforts were made by individuals in the final stages; Lord Oaksey and others ran in the London Marathon; Lord Abergavenny organized a sponsored ride in Kent to raise several thousand pounds; and the oldest member of the ground staff at Aintree made a sponsored bicycle ride round the course. A trainer gave his prize money to the Appeal, and others were holding open days at their stables, but this did not bring in much, as was illustrated when the famous Ian Balding raised only £755 at Kingclere. The Daily Express and other papers held contests, and the Aintree Clerk of the Course gave part of the royalties of a book, supported by his publishers. A raffle for a year's lease on a horse raised £130,000, an idea of trainer John Dunlop's. Another trainer, Pat Rowan, ran a raffle for cash prizes.

The question was bound to be asked, 'Who was to blame?' Was it the bookies, or the Jockey Club, or even the professional fund-raisers? There had of course been nothing incorrect in hiring a firm of professionals at nearly £1,000 a week to mastermind the Appeal. But the head fund-raiser himself seemed to feel he had not done as good a job as he ought, telling the press 'somehow I don't think we have got the seriousness of the situation across to the racing public' and took his share of the blame by saying, 'it is our fault'.

The Club did not have a clear strategy of what to do next, because, quite reasonably, no one wanted to talk about failure when their stance had to be one of a winner. There were a number of alternatives, of which the most favoured was to go to Davies and tell him that their best endeavours had secured less than the option figure, so, to put it bluntly, he could take it or leave it. This had always been the preferred position in the Club.

One thing the Jockey Club could not reasonably do was to back out of the whole thing, for reasons which are both logical and reasonable. First, the Jockey Club had made it clear from the moment that Lord Wigg put forward the proposal, that they supported the race. They wanted to save the Grand National. Furthermore, they set up the Appeal in such a way that they would not only organize the race, but effectively control it. As the people who were in control of racing in the United Kingdom, they wanted, they said, to see the National continue, despite the fact that many individual Club members, something like half, were indifferent or determinedly anti. And their racecourse-owning subsidiary took over management of the National very early in 1982.

So the Jockey Club was fully committed to the Appeal; there was no element of neutrality in public – with the one important exception that it would not put its own money forward in any great quantity. First of all it failed to raise the £½m from its own members, who were almost without exception rich by any normal definition, and would gain immensely, as Club members, by the acquisition of the race. Furthermore, as we have seen, it had assets in Newmarket Estates and Property Co. Limited, its subsidiary, which could most probably have been used to find the cash. But it was opposed to doing so, probably because so many members were ambivalent (at best) about the National. When the matter of a guarantee for the money was raised, Simon Weatherby said 'Newmarket Estates and Property Co. Limited could find the money, but they won't.'

Contrast the position in the Republic of Ireland, where the famous Dublin racecourse Phoenix Park needed £6m to be completely rehabilitated after it had fallen into disrepair and neglect. In a matter of months, a handful of rich directors, including Mr Robert Sangster, the pools millionaire, Mr Irwin of Goffs, Mr Mark Cavanagh and Mr Smurfitt, the entrepreneur, all set about raising the money, did so, and invested it in the course, including rebuilding the stands or completely refurbishing them. If they could do it, why, people asked, couldn't the Jockey Club, which had many more rich members, far ampler funds at its disposal.

It was predictable that the last thing the Jockey Club would do would be to find the shortfall from its own resources, its members or its subsidiaries. Instead, the senior steward rang Sir Ian Trethowan, the new head of the Levy Board, and told him that what had been informally agreed several weeks before must now be put on a formal footing, that was, that the Board would make a loan, probably interest-free. It was ironic that the betting public, having failed to give the £1½m which the Jockey Club had decided it should donate, had now to sit back and see £1m taken from it by levy handed over to the Club. Was this the sort of thing that Parliament had in mind when it set up the levy? There was in addition, the matter of the £¼m loaned to RHT to buy the option on the race.

So, with less than £1m in the bank, another £1m in promises, and the Levy Board's kind offer in his hip pocket, Johnny Henderson met Davies at Cheltenham and offered him £3m. Davies said his bankers wanted the other £1m within twelve months, and when Henderson refused to promise or guarantee this, Davies turned him down, although he gave him another ten days to find a further source of funds. Suggestions were coming in thick and fast.

Sam Vestey was away on a business trip while the various offers were analysed, but when the ten days came to an end, he returned in time to confront Davies at a secret meeting in the deserted weighing-in room at Cheltenham racecourse (near Vestey's home), where he was accompanied by Johnny Henderson and the Club Secretary, Christopher Foster. This time they had another £400,000 in the hip pocket which the Canadian whisky firm, Seagrams, had agreed to put 'up front' in a lump sum in return for a ten-year deal to sponsor the race, five years for a total of £700,000, plus an option for a further five years. By mid-afternoon, Davies and his bankers reluctantly agreed to take £3.4m – about what Aintree had cost him back in 1972. The Club was jubilant but still anxious, because they had not got £3.4m, even excluding the £1m loan from the Levy Board, and they were at some pains to 'remind' supporters that the £2.4m balance still relied partly on events and functions, which though scheduled and organized, had yet to take place. These included the Queen's offer to open the Royal Mews to the public in aid of the Appeal, and an Irish donation by Vincent O'Brien, Robert Sangster, and John Magnier, due in November, of an auctioned nomination (a service at stud to one of their best horses).

So the 1984 race was saved, and Murdoch's News International, which had sponsored it since 1975, stood down in favour of the new Seagram Grand National.

Why had the business of raising £4m been so tortuous? Was it that the racing public did not have sufficient zeal for the Aintree cause to want to save it? But with eleven million punters on the race every year, it seems hardly likely that they would not each give on average less than a pound to keep it. No, the answer must be that the Jockey Club had got it wrong, as the critics say it often does. Let there be no misunderstanding; the critics do not attack the Club only because it is full of Etonians and élitist, but because its performance leaves much to be desired, even in the areas where its expertise should be.

This criticism does not extend to the Club's administrators, Weatherby's, who are widely described as most efficient and technically competent, staffed and equipped as a modern business should be. This is not true of the Club, it is said. Just suppose that, stung to the quick by such criticism, the Club went on strike, it would be far from impossible to find a few dozen stout men to replace them and keep racing going, provided that Weatherby's took up a blackleg position. But being the kind of institution it is, one which the British racing public had, by and large, allowed to get away with heaven knows what over the years, could this group of well-meaning men and their advisers be blamed for getting the Appeal wrong? Perhaps not, but the outcome could be, amazingly, that the Club would actually consolidate its position of power over racing and racecourses, by adding to its crown one of the finest jewels from the Calendar, at virtually no cost.

The matter should certainly not rest there, because, to paraphrase the famous epigram, racing is far too serious a business to be left in the hands of the amateur. The present time is unlikely to be appropriate for a change. There are other priorities; the politicians in power have obvious reasons for doing nothing. But the day must surely come when enough is enough and a new way will be found. Meantime, long live the National, let it cease to be anybody's race and become everybody's, and let us enjoy our racing and leave its politics to the professionals.